Modi's Strategy for New India

Modi's Strategy for New India

Rajeev Ahuja

© Rajeev Ahuja 2022

All rights reserved.

No part of this book may be reproduced, or stored in a retrieval system, or transmitted in any form or by any means, electronic, mechanical, photocopying, recording, or otherwise, without express written permission of the Author.

ISBN: 979-84-2831-916-3

Cover page design by Ajay Rakha: arcreativewings@gmail.com ; Depiction of the Indian map is strictly for illustrative purpose only; Photo of Narendra Modi is taken from https://www.pmindia.gov.in/en/image-gallery/

To
my wife, Pooja, and children,
Harkrishna and Jeslyn.

Contents

Preface ix
Acknowledgments xi

1. Introduction 1
2. BJP's Aggressive Politics 13
3. A New Paradigm for a New India 25
4. Growth Vistas, New and Old 40
5. Tiny Tweaks 56
6. Push for Atmanirbhar Bharat 64
7. Good Governance 76
8. Narendra Damodardas Modi 87
9. Concluding Thoughts 95

End Notes 101

Preface

This book is the product of an entire year's effort between the winters of 2020 and 2021. In fact, the seeds were sown as early as 2015, when I gave up my full-time job to become a freelancer. Thereafter, I started following the Modi government's development policies and initiatives closely and began writing columns in national dailies. They were short pieces focused on specific topics. What was missing in those pieces was an overarching perspective on Modi's development strategy for India. That had to be a bigger and more serious undertaking.

The period of writing this book has been quite eventful. It saw the second and third COVID waves, another phase of lockdown, the vaccine roll-out, the ongoing farmers' protests, and some significant economic initiatives. The COVID crisis proved favourable for the writing of this book as consultancy opportunities dried up, which provided time (but not space!) to undertake this enterprise. Moreover, the COVID period provided a lot of insight as the government took significant measures to turn the crisis into an opportunity.

While home was the safest place to be during the pandemic, it was far from ideal from an author's perspective. Since my kids' online classes had turned our home into a virtual classroom, I had to move places to find solitude but also inspiration – which is so essential to keep the writing interest alive.

Some part of the writing was done out of my car. There were days I would drive to a quiet zone, park my car, open my laptop, and spend some time working on the book. The only thing I needed to ensure was that my laptop battery and my mind were adequately charged.

While writing the book, one thing that struck me was that whoever learnt about it was curious to know if the book was pro-Modi or anti-Modi. This would invariably be their first and foremost inquiry, regardless of their age, socio-economic background, or occupation. Such has been the impact of, and interest in, the Modi government.

It is only fair to mention that, had there been no coronavirus, this book probably wouldn't have taken shape. In all honesty, the timing of this book couldn't have been better; coming at a time when the country is celebrating Azadi Ka Amrit Mahotsav – a government initiative celebrating 75 years of India's independence.

Rajeev Ahuja
March 2022.

Acknowledgments

Through the journey of authoring this book, several friends helped me find the space I needed to write: NK Jain, Tanu Jain, Hazari Sethi, Ramesh Panwar, and Sudershana Jain in Shri Atma Vallabh Jain Smarak (Alipur, Delhi), Vijay Goel and Deepti Goel in Dadu Dayal Bhavan (Sonepat, Haryana), and Veerpal Singh in Deva Farms (Alipur, Delhi). I am grateful to all of them.

Of all these places, I spent the most time at Jain Smarak, which is remarkable for its simplicity and tranquillity. I was fortunate to be able to stay here, considering the residency is technically open only to those from the Jain sect. Gajender Kapri and his team in Bhojnalya took good care of my meals. The food they served was simple yet satisfying – something that I have started missing since. As an added bonus, I also got some orientation on Jainism. Dr. Mridula Jain, who works at the Smarak, was kind enough to give me that orientation.

Additionally, a few friends contributed by way of discussions and comments: C.S.C. Sekhar (Institute of Economic Growth), Meera Chatterjee (ex-World Bank colleague), Akshit Malhotra (Co-founder, Invisiobiome), Anurag Krishna (CSR division of TCS), and Amit Kumar (Consultant, Ministry of Finance). I am extremely grateful to them all. The book also benefitted from several rounds of discussion with an ex-IAS officer, who had the privilege of working at the PMO. I am indebted to this officer-friend, who wished to remain anonymous, for sharing his insights and enhancing my understanding of Indian politics. Last but not least, I am deeply grateful to Chitralekha Manohar (Founding Editor) and Diksha Devara (Editor, The Clean Copy) for their superb editing of the manuscript, to Abhishek Malhotra for giving ideas for the cover page, and to Sudhanshu Kanda for his guidance and support in getting the manuscript published.

1

༂༃

Introduction

Since Narendra Modi took over the reins at the centre, there have been sweeping changes – good, bad, extraordinary – in all domains, ranging across the social (e.g., enactment of the law against the social malpractice of triple talaq), cultural (e.g., enhanced bonding between regions[1]), economic (e.g., infrastructure development), geographic (e.g., heightened attention on smaller regions such as Leh and Ladakh), and political (use of central probe agencies to achieve political ambitions) realms. With so many changes being implemented, almost everyone has strong views on Narendra Modi and his administration.

Modi has attracted both blind followers (bhakts) and diehard critics. While bhakts attempt to find positives even in his missteps, critics seek out failings even in successful initiatives. Both the bhakts and the critics inevitably find themselves making mistakes in their analysis of the Modi administration, as its performance has so far been mixed.

Even educated professionals, who claim to be logical and fair in their assessments, fall prey to the same trap of selectively citing a few successes or failures depending on their political point of view. Such selectivity can hardly qualify as objectivity. Objectivity calls for analysing the government's performance in each domain individually rather than making sweeping statements.

In this context, it is important to set the record straight. To get a balanced perspective on the Modi government's performance, it's necessary to understand the larger game plan or strategy at work. This then is the objective of this short book – to examine the Modi administration's strategy and get a sense of its performance in the domain of economic development. While developments in other domains also matter, for an underdeveloped country like India, economic development is an overriding concern. Therefore, the focus of this book is on economic development exclusively.

It's no secret that PM Modi is highly ambitious about India's growth and development. He is a PM in a hurry. His government's development strategy revolves around achieving higher economic growth on a sustained basis. It has set for itself several ambitious targets to be achieved over the next few years and is striving towards them.

India has achieved substantial economic development under Modi's leadership. This claim may surprise, or even shock, his critics who believe otherwise. But there is plenty of evidence to suggest significant progress on the development front, as this book will show. But some thoughts on the strategy first.

The Modi government's strategy for India's development is different from that of its predecessors in two important ways: it is fast-paced and broad-based.

Fast-paced development

The Modi government has been pursuing fast-paced development, in tune with the changing times. The pace of economic activity overall has gone up. Governments everywhere need to run to stay in the same place, and if India intends to surge ahead, it needs to move faster. In addition, the rising expectations of people along with the huge developmental backlog have left the Modi government with no choice but to increase the pace of development. Technological changes that are aiding development processes are also fuelling people's aspirations. Having recognized India's development aspirations, challenges and potential, the Modi government has been enthusiastically working towards meeting its goals and speeding up development.

It is noticeable across the board that the pace of economic development has picked up under the Modi administration, which has been pursuing core economic reforms (relating to taxation, labour, agriculture, IT, etc.), building physical infrastructure (rail, roads, ports, airports), improving the business environment, providing additional support to certain industries (such as electronics, automobiles, defence, toys, and footwear), promoting innovation and technological change, and scaling up programmes that fulfil basic needs (housing for the poor, health security, cooking gas connections, drinking water, toilets, and so on). There is solid evidence in support of fast-paced development. It is not only about designing policies and programmes but also about implementing them to deliver on-ground results, i.e., translating intent into action. Anybody paying close attention to India's economic development over the years would have noticed a marked change in its pace.

However, fast-paced economic development has not translated into higher economic growth yet. But signs of positive change are already visible in some areas. In others, the change is yet to manifest at a scale required to move the growth needle. When economic development relates to foundational changes or systemic corrections, we will see results over time. When the moves are unerring, positive results are bound to follow.

Broad-based development

Acknowledging India's inherent strengths – its people, natural resources, cultures, and languages – the Modi government has been pursuing a broad-based development strategy. This allows India to capitalize on its intrinsic strengths and new opportunities, which are essential for long-term, sustained economic growth. A broad-based strategy can generate economic growth across all sectors of society. Every household must participate in and consequently benefit from the process.

Several programmes of the Modi government are aimed at generating broad-based development. As discussed further, programmes such as the Atal Innovation Mission (2016), Startup India (2016), Stand-Up India (2016), Mudra Yojana (2015), and many more are all aimed at promoting innovation and entrepreneurship, especially among women and the youth. The government has introduced initiatives targeting previously neglected and underdeveloped regions of the country, such as the north-eastern region, Jammu and Kashmir, Ladakh, the coastal belts, and so on. Similarly, several steps have been taken to encourage the spread of micro, small, and medium enterprises (MSMEs) in different regions. The agricultural sector, which employs a sizeable labour force, has seen a series of reforms aimed at doubling farmers' incomes.

Several welfare interventions aimed at meeting basic needs (housing, health security, clean water, toilet, food, and life skills) acquire a different interpretation when seen from the lens of broad-based development. By empowering people, welfare interventions allow people to partake in the development process. A higher pace of development is also evident in the provision of these basic facilities.

A slogan coined by the Modi government highlights this idea of broad-based development: *Sab Ka Saath, Sab Ka Vikas, Sab Ka Vishwash, Sab Ka Prayas*. In other words, to promote general development, the government needs active effort, support, and trust from its people.

Broad-based development may suggest a lack of prioritization. However, this stance is incorrect as some broad prioritization can be discerned. For example, the education sector didn't receive as much attention as the health sector during the first term. Similarly, the push that Swachh Bharat Abhiyan (Clean India Mission) received in the first term, Jal Jeevan Abhiyan (Drinking Water Mission) started to receive only from the second term. Prioritization exists not only across sectors but within sectors too. The speed of development is dictated not by the absence of preparation or planning but by limitations on the capacity to further development.

To achieve fast-paced and broad-based development, the Modi government has been following a development approach characterized by the following attributes.

Working on several fronts

Fast-paced development requires the government to work simultaneously on multiple fronts; the Modi government is constantly dealing with varied development challenges.

Despite several obstacles hindering the development agenda, the Modi government seems undeterred. Electoral cycles have not stood in the way of bold reforms (e.g., the Goods and Services Tax reforms [GST]), the benefits of which accrue in the medium term but entail short-term difficulties. Additionally, it has actively pursued unfinished projects that were initiated by its predecessors; though this may have been to gain credibility in the eyes of the public, several of these ventures have proved successful. Similarly, vested interests have not deterred the Modi government from taking the reforms agenda forward. For example, proposing the (in)famous three farm laws to reform agricultural markets in the country or the scrapping of the Medical Council of India -- a highly influential body that controlled medical education in the country – and replacing it with the National Medical Commission. While strong vested interests in the agricultural sector forced the Modi administration to step back on the farm laws, those that controlled medical education were successfully defeated.

Problem-solving approach

The Modi government advocates comprehensive problem-solving rather than superficial attempts. The thorough mindset of the government is discernible from its completion of some projects ahead of time or in record time, which is rare in government projects. For example, the target of the Ujjawala scheme (2016), to provide free cooking gas (LPG) connections to 50 million poor households by March 31, 2019, was met ahead of time. Likewise, the target of electrifying all un-electrified villages was achieved within a record time of 1,000 days of PM Modi making this announcement. More recently, the work of constructing the Defence Offices Complex (in Delhi) was completed in only 12 months as against its scheduled completion in 24 months. These examples are not meant to suggest that there have been no delays in project completion. Instead, these examples of positive deviance create a "new normal" of government functioning.

Furthermore, Modi's administration believes in solving problems holistically as opposed to treating them as standalone. The recognition of interrelationships and interconnections in the design and sequencing of the proposed development interventions is evident. For example, inclusive banking through Jan Dhan Yojana preceded the full-fledged implementation of direct benefit transfers under various schemes. Likewise, primacy was given to reforming the Indian medical education system, the root of any major expansion in the delivery of healthcare.

Seizing emerging opportunities

The Modi government is seeking to exploit India's economic potential without losing sight of emerging opportunities. It is not only working to complete projects in India's unfinished development agenda but also opening up new vistas for the country's development. On one hand, it is fighting the challenges of poverty and malnutrition, and on the other, it is venturing into unchartered territories such as the deep ocean and space exploration.

Keeping an eye on emerging growth opportunities, the government is working on the development of inland waterways, making India a global hub for the production and export of green hydrogen, turning India into a start-up hub, transforming its automotive sector through a shift towards electric mobility, facilitating an energy transition away from fossil fuels to using renewables, and much more. This diversity is what makes the Modi government stand out.

Another instance is the promotion of innovation and research by the government. Its efforts in this direction are expected to take India far up the ladder. India has already achieved the status of being the world's third-largest start-up hub following the US and China. With sustained efforts, India will no doubt be a huge player in offering sustainable solutions to the rest of the world.

If the Modi government is promoting economic development like never before, then why are so many people critical of it?

Through its conduct, the Modi government has made many enemies. Any political party remaining in power over consecutive terms tends to generate restlessness within the opposition; and when the party in power has ambitious goals and uses any means to stay in power, it is bound to turn political adversaries into enemies. Hence, having political rivals is understandable.

Outside of politics too, Modi has many adversaries. Some people in disagreement with the politics of the Modi government have turned critical of everything his government does. However, there is a lot to be critical of the Modi government in terms of politics rather than economics. In fact, on the development front, his government has put up a pretty impressive show. Some new adversaries, however, have emerged as a direct result of Modi's new governance model. By introducing greater accountability in the delivery of public services and the distribution of public subsidies, he has deprived 'middlemen' of their income. These middlemen, who were accustomed to shortcuts, are against the Modi government now that avenues for commissions and kickbacks have dried up.

Some people who have been adversely affected by the economic policies of the government, despite rapid economic development, remain critical. Any economic reform creates winners and losers. The losers, who think only of their self-interest, will not be happy with the government. Such people may be numerous when the costs of economic reform are spread over a large section of society (as with the introduction of the Goods and Services Tax). Making systemic corrections does entail pain during a transition phase. Those who have been adversely affected during this phase have reason to complain. But their complaints too may be transitory, as these same people will potentially benefit from the new opportunities that emerge.

Some professionals, including economists and domain experts, are critical of the Modi government either because it has ignored them or their professional advice. Alternatively, their professional duplicity has been exposed either due to their contradictory stances or lack of professional integrity. These people tend to turn a blind eye to the 'big picture' in sight of which these public decisions are made. Raghuram Rajan (former RBI governor) and Arvind Subramaniam (former Chief Economic Advisor) who once occupied top government positions but have now turned into its critics are examples of this.

Some development experts continue to find fault even with successful government initiatives such as Digital India, Pradhan Mantri Jan Swasthya Yojana, Swachh Bharat Abhiyan, and Ujjwala Yojana. Still, there is scope for improvement, and progressive refinement is an ongoing affair. There are also activists opposed to the 'development model' of the Modi government. People who value environmental or cultural preservation more than economic growth are opposed to initiatives like palm tree cultivation in the Andaman and Nicobar Islands and the north-eastern region, transforming the Lakshadweep into a tourist destination, and privatization of public-sector enterprises.

Domain experts who are unhappy with the progress taking place in their specific domain are critical of the Modi government, as reforms in certain areas such as education and power sector have indeed been slow.

There are some idealists and critics who will condemn the government regardless of who is in power. The Modi government is no exception. Their fight is for certain principles. Little do they appreciate that development is all about pragmatism and making compromises.

While some choose to passively defame the government, others may resort to more aggressive approaches such as misrepresenting facts and painting a bleak picture. Unfortunately, this has become an industry of its own, used as much by the government to counter it as by the people who propagate it.

Regardless of how powerful, educated, well-connected, and strategic these critics are, they form a minority. Modi remains a popular leader both within and outside of India. There has to be something substantive that leads to his popularity. Could it be his government's development performance?

Structure of the book

The book is organized into eight chapters. *Chapter two* is all about the BJP's politics, which is essential to understanding Modi's development paradigm. By providing insights into the tricks and tactics that the BJP has been playing in the political arena, this chapter puts the BJP's politics into perspective. There is a lot to be critical of the BJP's politics, but to Modi, it is the means to achieving the end of having a more successful Indian economy. The end justifies using all means – 'right' or 'wrong' – to insulate the development trajectory from the compulsions of political cycles.

The Modi government's development strategy is focused on democratizing growth by unleashing the power of India's people, harnessing the power of technology, and opening up new vistas for growth. India's populace is at the core of the Modi government's development strategy. The various development programmes of his government revolve around unlocking citizens' entrepreneurial spirit, building capabilities, and providing a supportive ecosystem. *Chapter three* gets into the 'whys' and the 'hows' of these key ideas.

Chapter four is about new vistas for growth. With a renewed emphasis on traditional growth drivers such as agriculture and

MSMEs, India can achieve higher growth. To realize aspirational double-digit growth, however, India must open up new avenues for growth. Whether it's the energy transition away from fossil fuels towards renewables, investing in waterways to lower logistics costs, enabling electric mobility, or adding new destinations and improving connectivity for the promotion of tourism, the Modi government has been systematically working on opening these new growth avenues.

Chapter five provides examples of tiny tweaks that stand testament to the Modi government's attention to detail. Even as the administration has been engaged in taking big and bold economic decisions, it hasn't ignored numerically smaller groups – they are being attended to alongside major economic transformations. For instance, amending the Indian Forest Act 1927 to allow harvesting of bamboo in non-forest areas to enhance the earnings of rural and forest dwellers dependent on bamboo for their livelihood or the construction of the Matri Setu bridge connecting Tripura with Bangladesh to boost economic activities, particularly among the producers of bamboo products and pineapple in Tripura.

Chapter six examines the Modi government's recent Atmanirbhar Bharat or Self-reliant India campaign (2020). This chapter brings out the core idea of Atmanirbhar Bharat Abhiyan as well as the confusion around it. The core idea of Atmanirbhar Bharat, or Self-reliant India, may be the need of the hour in the current post-COVID economic reality, but the government's definition of it and the accompanying narrative has gone a little haywire. Separating substance from the chaff, this chapter dwells on the rationale as well as the debate around it.

Chapter seven is about good governance – one of the main planks on which the Modi government came to power in 2014. Once in power, the government took some decisive steps to benefit investors and the business community alike. Civil society too has benefitted from improved governance. However, in a few other areas of governance, such as the functioning of public institutions, there is much criticism against the ruling dispensation. This chapter highlights a few examples of success as well as areas of heated controversy.

Chapter eight is on Narendra Modi himself. This chapter provides a peek into Modi's personality and his method of functioning. Understanding Modi along these dimensions is important to gain an appreciation of the Modi government's decision-making. Modi's passion and ambitions for India's development, his hard-working ethos, his openness to experimentation, and his belief in action over discussion, is reflected in his governance style. He has deep insights into politics as well as into development processes and understands the complex relationship between these two worlds.

Chapter nine, the last chapter, contains some concluding thoughts.

2

BJP's Aggressive Politics

2014 proved to be a significant year for Indian politics. At the national level, the BJP-led NDA government came to power on the planks of anti-corruption and development. Capitalizing on the bruised reputation of the UPA-2 government along with a string of scams and unfortunate incidents, the NDA roundly defeated the UPA-2 at the hustings.

Since then, the political landscape in India has changed forever. Besides the expansion of its base, BJP has also altered the raison d'être for being a politician: it is no longer about the individual participating but about society and nation-building. These changes are noticeable at the national and state levels already.

Once in power, the BJP has been pursuing aggressive politics with considerable success. Its political strategy has helped the party achieve 'Mission Lotus' – that is, expand its base in many states either directly or by forming alliances with local parties.[2] It also succeeded in getting re-elected at the centre in 2019 and is hoping to stay in power for many more terms.

Political power accrues to those that outsmart the rest. The BJP, with Narendra Modi at its helm, has proved to be the smartest of them all. To achieve its political ambitions, it has been playing several tricks: some well-known and others not-so-well-known but all played well to its advantage. So, what are these tricks?

Playing politics of 'vote banks' and development

For a long time, political parties in India have played 'vote bank' politics – that is, politics that appeals not to individual citizens but groups and sub-groups based on their identities defined by religion, caste, class, and region.[3] Such divisive politics have had a strong influence on political parties' success in elections. No political party aspiring to come to power can afford to ignore such divisive politics, and the BJP has proven to be a master at this. However, where it differs from other political parties is how it plays the 'vote bank' card. It is more analytical and strategic; it plays this card more in its electoral management strategy than in its narrative.

It has also been playing the politics of development as there are limits to divisive politics. India has a diverse populace and aspiring Indians want real development that can help them realize their dreams and ambitions. The Modi government has brought development issues to the centre stage of Indian politics and converted this into electoral wins. Indeed, the Modi government's track record of fast-paced, broad-based development, and its clever marketing of these policies among the populace, is unmatched. It is BJP's commitment to development, and not corruption, that often finds mention in electoral campaigns.

In a mature society, the electorate supports political parties based on their vision for development, values, and stance on social issues. In such a society, party appeals are truly inclusive and directed at citizens, not groups. This level of electoral maturity will take a long time to establish in a nation like India. Till then, parties will continue to play 'vote bank' politics alongside the politics of development, while the Modi government has been playing both cards for electoral gains all along.

Weakening the opposition

BJP as a political organization derives its strength from the support of the cadre of its ideological parent, RSS (Rashtriya Swayamsevak Sangh). It has also benefited from the lack of a strong opposition. The BJP must continuously strive to weaken the opposition, which is integral to realizing Mission Lotus.

Using central probe agencies – targeting selectively

Indeed, the Modi government has been playing several tricks and tactics to weaken the opposition. For example, it has used central probe agencies to selectively target opposition leaders who are perceived to be a threat to this government. Sample this.

P. Chidambaram, a senior Congress leader, has been one of the most vocal critics of the Modi government. On August 21, 2019, he was arrested dramatically by the Central Bureau of Investigation in connection with a corruption and money laundering case, hours after the Supreme Court refused to grant an immediate hearing on his plea for interim protection from arrest. The Congress accused the government of targeting opposition leaders and termed the action of probe agencies as a "political vendetta". P. Chidambaram alleged that the investigation agency was "acting on the behest of the centre" as he is a political opponent of government in power. His son, Karti Chidambaram, termed it as an attempt to silence one of the most vocal critics of the government.

Indirectly referring to Chidambaram's arrest, Raghuram Rajan, a noted economist and a former RBI governor, commented,[4] "It's unclear why evaders are problematic only in the opposition and not in members of the opposition who pledge allegiance to the ruling party."

Using central probe agencies – getting the timings right

In the targeting of selective persons, the BJP can time it well. Sample this.

When the 2019 general elections were just a couple of months away, a central probe agency for the first time interrogated an extended member of the Gandhi family. Robert Vadra – businessman and Sonia Gandhi's son-in-law – appeared before a central probe agency in connection with alleged criminal charges of dubious financial dealings. Vadra had denied those allegations in the past and termed them a 'political witch hunt' against him. With Vadra in the agencies' net, the Modi government played "no tolerance to corruption" card whereas the Congress simply questioned: "why just before elections". Just days earlier to this incident, Priyanka Gandhi Vadra had made her official entry into politics.

Close to the heels of this incident, Sonia Gandhi, UPA's chairperson said, "Bluff, bluster, and intimidation have been Modi government's philosophy."

Using tactics of fear and intimidation

BJP is also good at creating fear to put psychological pressure on opposition leaders. Here is an example.

West Bengal (WB) Chief Minister, Mamata Banerjee, refused to give her speech at an event on her home turf (Kolkata) in the presence of PM Modi. The event was organized by the central government to celebrate Netaji Subhas Chandra Bose's birth anniversary. As soon as she was called on the stage to address the gathering a section of the crowd started making noise and started shouting slogans such as "Jai Shri Ram" and "Modi-Modi". Feeling insulted, she refused to give her speech. She said that the dignity of government programmes must be maintained because such events are not of any one political party. This incident happened when the WB state assembly elections were just a couple of months away.

Funding of elections

Another trick deployed to weaken the opposition is hitting where it hurts most, that is, political funding. The government did not squarely address the issue of political funding, which has a significant bearing on parties winning and losing elections. State funding of elections could bring some parity among parties in the funding of election campaigns and also check 'commercialization' of elections. The government, however, informed the Parliament that the Election Commission of India (ECI) was not in favour of state funding of elections due to its inability to prohibit or check candidates' own expenditure over and above that provided by states.[5]

However, the government did introduce the Electoral Bonds Scheme in 2018. But before doing so, the government covertly made four crucial amendments to four different acts in the Finance Bill, 2017. The ECI sharply criticized these amendments, terming it a "retrograde step" that would open up a loophole for routing black money. Rather than addressing the long-standing issue of introducing transparency in political funding, the scheme appears to be adding to the problem. Even the RBI had raised concerns regarding the electoral bonds. Incidentally, the BJP turned out to be the biggest beneficiary of Rs 6,493 crore worth of electoral bonds sold in three years.[6]

In his conversation with the Harvard Kennedy School Ambassador, Nicholas Burns, Rahul Gandhi mentioned that the BJP has absolute dominance over finances and media and that he doesn't have the structure needed to run a political party.[7]

Power poaching

The BJP weakens the party in power and then capitalizes on its weaknesses. This power poaching game goes on all the time. Sample this.

On March 20, 2020, Madhya Pradesh Chief Minister, Kamal Nath, resigned from the top post as his government fell short of the majority mark. Around 15 months after taking office, Nath's government plunged into crisis when 22 state legislators rebelled against him. What triggered this rebellion was the former union minister and senior Congress leader Jyotiraditya Scindia's decision to quit the Congress and join the BJP. Before meeting the governor, Nath held a press conference blaming the BJP for conspiring against his government. Nath said, "BJP has been trying to pull down our government since day one. Our MLAs were made hostage in Bengaluru. People will know the truth of BJP soon…"

Madhya Pradesh was not the only state where the defection of MLAs led to the fall of the government. In the recent past, Manipur, Goa, Arunachal Pradesh, and Karnataka also met the same fate because of the defection by MLAs. As per a report by the Association for Democratic Reforms, 44 percent of MLAs across states who switched parties joined the BJP in the last five years.[8]

Weakening of public institutions

Sometimes, even heads of public institutions become targets for such tactics. Here is an example of the modus operandi used by the government to intimidate the Chief Information Commissioner's office.

India's Right to Information (RTI) Act, 2005, is one of the most advanced and powerful pieces of rights legislation in the world. Some people have accused the BJP government of taking measures to compromise the implementation of RTI Act. For example, a former Chief Information Commissioner, M. Sridhar Acharyulu, in his letter to the President of India on December 4, 2018, wrote that Information Commissioners are being "legally" intimidated to prevent them discharging their legal duties. How? By filing hundreds of frivolous writ petitions against the CIC just because the latter ordered disclosure of information buried under sarkari files under the RTI Act.[9]

Getting the chief of a public institution to toe the line lends some advantages to the ruling dispensation. The ECI has been accused several times of being biased, undemocratic, and selective in penalizing violators of the Model Code of Conduct. Commenting on the BJP's style of functioning, a well-known politician remarked, "[Under Modi's rule] institutions have been subverted. Political opponents have been hounded. Dissent has been suppressed. Freedom of speech – the most basic of all freedoms – have been sought to be curtailed and silenced."

At times, changes in constitutional provisions may be necessary. The BJP-led government doesn't shy away from implementing these changes. For example, in July 2019, the Modi government amended the Right to Information Act, 2005, which seeks to bring transparency and accountability to government functioning. According to the amendments, the Chief Information Commissioner

(CIC) and Information Commissioners (ICs) may no longer enjoy five-year tenures and perks – similar to those of the Chief Election Commissioner (CEC) and Election Commissioners (ECs) – as allowed under the RTI Act. Some opposition leaders accused the government of diluting the effectiveness of the Act as it leaves the CIC office to the mercy of the very government it is supposed to hold accountable.

It seems that the BJP government will go to any extent to remove hurdles that come in its way. Former Vice President, Hamid Ansari, provides some insight into this in his recent book, *By Many a Happy Accident*.[10] He mentions that as the Vice President, he was also the Chairman of the Rajya Sabha when the BJP lacked the required arithmetic to get bills passed. In a surprising turn of events, PM Modi approached him in his chamber and questioned him as to why he wasn't allowing bills to be passed in the Rajya Sabha. Modi made the assertion, and authoritatively so, that the BJP's majority coalition gave it a moral right to prevail over procedural impediments. Although this instance relates to parliamentary business, the BJP's political conduct is not different; it doesn't hesitate to bypass established rules, protocols, processes to advance its agenda. Some custodians fight to safeguard against such violations while others play to the government's tune. When public institutions are headed by pliable officers, the government gets its way. There is a Hindi saying which goes "*Jab saiya bhai kotwal to ab dar kahe ka*" – if your husband (or partner) is a police officer, then why be scared. Of course, the pliable officers get fittingly rewarded. For example, some observers believe that the nomination of a former Chief Justice of India (CJI), Rajan Gogoi, to the Rajya Sabha barely four months after his retirement was a matter of quid pro quo. When Rajan Gogoi was CJI, he allocated and handled key cases – the Rafale matter, the Ayodhya matter, and a few other cases in which the government had a major political stake.[11] His nomination raised a big question mark regarding the judiciary's independence.

All the above tricks can be connected to a time-tested strategy of *saam* (to cajole), *daam* (to purchase), *dand* (to punish), and *bhed* (to exploit weaknesses).[12] These four ways – in increasing order of harshness – are liberally deployed by the BJP as a means of manipulation. This is not only to weaken the opposition but also to make various public institutions comply with its diktat. In short, the BJP is using every means to achieve what it wants to, politically.

The more challenging the opposition, the more aggressive the BJP gets. In Hindi, there is a saying, "*Tu ser tho main sava ser*", which means "I will always be one up on you". The aggressiveness of the BJP's politics is a function of the strength of the challenge thrown at it by the opposition.

Anticipating a tough fight during the 2019 general elections, PM Modi launched a big scheme, Pradhan Mantri Kisan Samman Nidhi Yojana (PM Kisan), just a couple of months before the elections. The scheme guarantees an income of Rs 6,000 annually, payable in three instalments of Rs 2,000 each, to over 120 million small and marginal farmers across India. PM Kisan was purposely launched in UP, as the state comprised the maximum number of 21.4 million farmers or nearly 18% of beneficiaries. The state also has the maximum number of Lok Sabha seats (80).

Some opposition leaders termed it as a 'bribe for votes'. A pre-election survey indicated that the PM Kisan scheme was one of the three decisions of the Modi government that had the ability to change the course of the 2019 election.[13] Indeed, the BJP and its allies won 64 of the 80 seats in the state despite the odds being hopelessly stacked against them.

Playing the nationalist card

The Modi government doesn't shy away from playing the 'nationalist card'. In response to the Pulwama terror attack, believed to have been engineered by a Pakistan-based terror outfit, the Modi government conducted an airstrike in the town of Balkot in Pakistan. Before the 2019 general elections, Rahul Gandhi accused the BJP of creating a hyper-nationalistic environment. Some political observers believe that the airstrike had created a favourable perception of Prime Minister Modi and this contributed to the BJP's win in the elections just a couple of months after the retaliatory airstrike.

Being street-smart

BJP is street-smart with its tricks. For example, the Coronavirus vaccine certificate bears PM Modi's photo along with a message, and the boarding pass of the former state-owned carrier, Air India, again carried PM Modi's photo. These moves invited criticism from the opposition during assembly elections. When opposition parties complained to the ECI citing a violation of the code of conduct, it directed the removal of the photos. Still, the BJP used the opportunity to advance 'brand Modi' even if only for a brief intervening period.

Using narratives and dramatics to its advantage

The BJP is a master crafter in spinning narratives and using all its channels to relay them. This can have varied purposes: to taunt the opposition, find faults, indulge in a blame game, distract public attention, inform/remind the public of the government's achievements, and so forth. It smartly dips into archives and pulls out snippets to show the opposition and its leaders in poor light.

They also coined a powerful slogan, *Sab Ka Saath Sab Ka Vikas*, which was later revised to *Sab Ka Saath, Sab Ka Vikas, Sab Ka Vishwash, Sab Ka Prayas*. Even the slogan "*Jai Jawan Jai Kisan*" –

coined by the second Prime Minister of India, Lal Bahadur Shastri – has been improved upon to read *"Jai Jawan, Jai Kisan, Jai Vigyan."* Its large repertoire of slogans often catches people's attention, along with its association with multiple sectors spanning sports, film, etc. For example, PM Modi cited India's win in a cricket test match series to say that the 'Atmanirbhar Bharat' mission has spread to all sectors and walks of society.

Watching Indian politics today is no less interesting than following a blockbuster with action-packed scenes, drama, comedy, and thrilling sequences. Using all of these tactics, the BJP-led government has turned itself into a formidable force that cannot be defeated by any political party alone. The opposition parties must unite to take on the Modi-led BJP government. Even then, it is a challenge as the BJP cannot be combatted through regular politics.

Discussion

Electoral victories are all about winning the hearts and minds of the public. It is also about strategizing well: forging alliances, fielding candidates, conducting deep data analytics to identify seats that can be won, devising appropriate campaign strategies, and so forth. In other words, electoral wins are about doing whatever it takes to woo voters and strategizing to win the most seats. If it's nationalism that appeals to voters, play the nationalist card; if it's divisive politics that appeals to sub-groups of voters, play that card; if it's real development that moves the educated, go all out for it; if it's cash that gets votes, figure out a legitimate way to provide it. Nothing is unfair if it's done within legal and constitutional boundaries, and it is necessary to push boundaries in politics.

Politics is dirty, messy, and devoid of ethics or morality. It is only about lawful and unlawful conduct, and even this can be manipulated. There is a saying which goes, "all is fair in love and war;

and political battle is nothing less than a war." The quest for being in power is so strong that whoever is at the helm tends to misuse government machinery to further their political agenda. This is true not just of political parties but of politicians too. Today's foes become friends tomorrow, and tomorrow's friends turn into foes again. It's all situational. There is a Hindi proverb which goes "*Jaise sampnath vaise nagnath*" – meaning both (or all) are the same, only the scale changes. The BJP has clearly surpassed the scale seen in the past, which is why some people dislike its politics.

What really matters is not what goes on in the political arena or how electoral battles are fought. In the ancient Indian epic, the Mahabharata, Lord Krishna recommends the use of deceitful and immoral strategies in the service of moral causes. The ends justify the means when major issues [development and progress] are at stake. So, what matters is: what does any party do once it comes to power? What is its raison d'etre of being in power? Is it working for the larger good of society? In a development-hungry nation like India, is the government working towards progress? This then is the central question to which the rest of the book is devoted.

3

A New Paradigm for a New India

More ambitious than any goal set for India before, PM Modi has set a target of achieving a GDP of $5 trillion by 2024–25. This translates to almost doubling the size of the economy in a span of five years (2019–20 to 2024–25).[14] Although the government had made previous references to the goal, it was not until the *Economic Survey 2018–19* that the first official blueprint of the goal was outlined.[15] This goal requires India's economy to grow at an average annual rate of 8 percent every year beginning 2019–20, which is challenging. However, achieving this target has become more daunting due to the coronavirus pandemic that has been ravaging the global economy since early 2020.

The goal received mixed reactions. A former finance minister, P. Chidambaram, downplayed the goal stating that India would be able to achieve the goal through natural progression. He stated that an economy that grows nominally at 11% per annum will double in six years, regardless of who the PM or FM is. This is simply the power of compounding.[16] However, a former PM, Manmohan Singh, considered the goal to be wishful thinking.[17] Both are senior Congress leaders with differing views on the 5T goal. In retaliation, Modi termed his critics "professional pessimists". In his view, there should be debate and criticism on the ways and means of achieving the goal rather than questioning the goal itself.[18]

Admittedly, this overarching goal is more aspirational than strategic. Even so, it did provide a singular focus to experts both within and outside the government. Calculating the contributions of varying sectors and mapping the potential of different industries allowed for the creation of state-wise targets. For example, Uttar Pradesh started aiming to become a trillion-dollar economy by 2024–25. The central government has been working in tandem with stakeholders – states, the private sector, or civil society – to achieve the goal, as it cannot do it alone. Never before has the country evaluated its economic potential along these lines; such is the power of having an ambitious goal.

Many are reconsidering the feasibility of the goal following the COVID pandemic. India's growth is expected to be impacted by this global crisis, but the *Economic Survey 2020–21*, which was released almost a year into the pandemic, does not mention it. The survey notes that 90 percent of countries are expected to experience contraction as a result of the COVID-19 pandemic. Yet, it fails to acknowledge its impact on the 5T goal.[19]

Officially, the goal has remained constant, and it was restated in 2019 and 2021. However, whatever slim chance India had for achieving the goal has been dimmed by the pandemic. Internally, the government perhaps recognizes the setback caused by COVID-19, but it is still hopeful of achieving the goal a year or two later.[20] This hope rests on a series of economic reforms that it has unleashed and various development programmes that it has rolled out. Also, the Modi government's push for an Atmanirbhar Bharat (Self-reliant India) aims at converting this adversity into an opportunity. India is seeking to play a greater role in global supply chains that stand disrupted due to COVID-19 and to reduce its import dependence by promoting make-in-India (see chapter #6). It remains to be seen how long India takes to achieve the 5T goal.

COVID-19 has dented but not debilitated the Indian economy. India's prospects of emerging to be the fastest growing economy in the world remain intact. As for the immediate economic outlook, some experts are debating the shape of India's economic recovery (U-shaped, V-shaped, K-shaped), while leading international organizations (IMF, World Bank, ADB) have revised their projections for India's growth rate. These experts and organizations largely focus on short-term economic growth – quarterly or even annually. They need to look at India's growth within the wider development context.

A new paradigm

A significant shift in the development paradigm and a structural transformation of the Indian economy are underway. This is necessary for India to achieve higher growth on a sustained basis over the medium to longer term. Focusing on short-term growth at the expense of underlying shifts and transformations could be misleading. It is important to recognize that the Modi government is attempting to prepare the economy for the long haul. That is, for the sustained high growth that India is capable of achieving.

India's story of economic growth can be explained using a simple example.

Suppose there are two routes to go from point A (the origin) to point B (the destination): a short route that is 300 km long and an alternate route that is 350 km long. On the short route, one can travel at a uniform speed of 50 km per hour. So, it takes 6 hours to cover the distance of 300 km. On the alternate route, the initial 50 km is covered at a uniform speed of 25 km per hour but the remaining 300 km can be covered at a uniform speed of 100 km per hour. So, it takes a total of 5 hours to make the journey on the alternate route. Even though the alternate route is longer, you get to the destination sooner than on the short route. This is shown in the diagram below. This example demonstrates that under certain 'conditions', the longer route can get us to the destination faster. Of course, the results are sensitive to the assumptions made. Changing these assumptions can get us different results.

Diagram 1: Two different routes

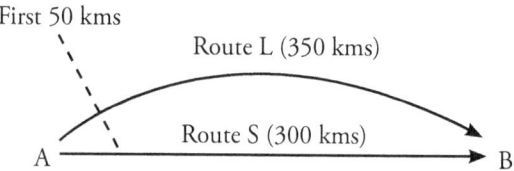

Route S is covered in 6 hrs at uniform speed of 50 km/hr
Route L is covered in 5 hrs:
  (i) first 50 km covered in 2 hrs at a uniform spped of 25 km/hr
  (ii) the remaining 300 km covered in 3 hrs at a unifom speed of 100 km/hr

How is this example relevant here? This example explains India's growth story quite well. The two routes in the diagram represent two different paradigms: the straight route represents the conventional paradigm while the curved route represents the new paradigm. These two paradigms differ in terms of the time taken to realize India's growth aspiration. While the conventional paradigm delivers steady growth, stellar performance comes from the new paradigm.

Broad-based development represents a new paradigm. It has the potential to speed up growth but only over the medium to long term. However, it entails short-term costs in terms of a slow-down in growth in the initial phase. The initial phase is a preparatory phase for the new paradigm. Once fully activated, the economy will receive a huge boost and start accelerating. Because economic growth is a long-term play, any strategy that speeds up growth during this period is superior to one that keeps it stagnant. This simple logic is captured in the diagram above.

If the horizon is short term, the conventional paradigm does better; but if this horizon is stretched to a longer term, it is the new paradigm that does better. Another way to understand this is through the bamboo and fern analogy. The fern grows surprisingly fast in contrast to bamboo, which shows no activity for the first few years, but that doesn't mean the bamboo isn't growing. Initially, all the bamboo growth happens underneath, which is crucial for it to grow tall when it grows above the surface. Those who are eager to see green shoots are in for disappointment in the short term as they miss out on the development underneath.

A framework for broad-based growth

To turn India into a global economic powerhouse like China, growth must emanate from every stratum of society. The Modi government's broad-based development strategy takes a people-centric approach, to enable the population to grow and achieve their aspirations. India's population is a potential asset on both the demand and supply sides. Not only does it form a huge market, but it can also be a part of increasing supply – harnessing this potential can help reinforce both production and consumption.

Diagram 2: People-centric development

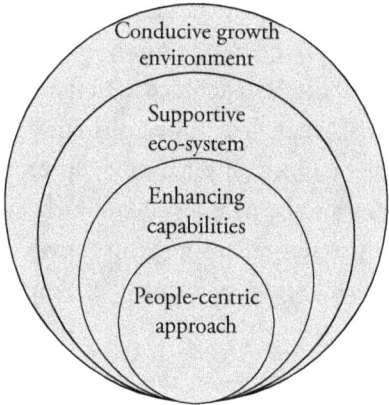

On the contrary, failing to tap this potential would mean missing out on potential economic benefits. Additionally, it can turn people into a liability for the government in more ways than one – not only in terms of providing social security benefits but also in preventing the social unrest that the young populace is capable of creating. Hence, the merits of the government's people-centric approach to growth and development must be seen against this backdrop.

The Modi government has rolled out several new and revamped programmes to realize India's human resource potential, especially that of women and youth. They are designed to provide knowledge, skills, and credit to achieve their goals. These programmes provide a supportive ecosystem that enables partnerships and reduces the burden of compliance (refer to diagram 2).

In the past, India did not emphasize science, technology, research, and innovation as it ought to have. For example, in 1996, India and

China were at comparable levels in their spending on research and development.[21] Over the years, China has surged ahead of India. The Modi government has been making sincere efforts to correct this distortion by promoting innovation and entrepreneurship. This is evident in several of its programmes such as the Atal Innovation Mission (AIM), Startup India, Women Entrepreneurship Platform, Stand-Up India, Mudra Yojana, and so forth.

Atal Innovation Mission (AIM), which aims at inculcating scientific inquiry among students and promoting problem-solving capabilities, is one such impactful programme. Atal tinkering labs are set up in schools to promote scientific curiosity, and Atal incubator centres are established in universities/institutions to foster start-ups. Emphasis is given to finding innovative solutions to societal needs in addition to creating a national network of mentors and building partnerships with various agencies.

Similarly, Startup India aims to nurture innovation and start-ups in the country by building a strong ecosystem. The programme is expected to drive economic growth and generate employment opportunities. It promotes start-ups in a wide array of sectors by simplifying procedures and thereby reducing compliance burdens, enabling knowledge exchange and access to funding, and fostering industry–academia partnerships and incubation. The government launched the Startup India Seed Fund to provide funding and employment opportunities, particularly in tier 2 and 3 towns of India. The fund aims to provide financial assistance to start-ups at every stage, from proof of concept, prototype development, product trials, and market entry to commercialization.

Having started in 2016, both the programmes have helped drive significant progress. Over a dozen start-ups have already launched out of the tinkering labs. Around 50 incubators are operational and are supporting around 1,200 start-ups. AIM's initiatives have played an important contributory role in advancing India's position in the Global Innovation Index from 81 in 2015 to 48 in 2020.

Between Jan 2016 and Dec 2020, over 41,000 start-ups have been recognized by the Department of Promotion of Industry and Internal Trade (DPIIT). Almost 30 states and UTs have a dedicated start-up policy. Over 590 districts have at least one start-up. Over Rs 4,500 crore of investments has been made in nearly 400 start-ups through a fund of fund scheme.[22] Even if a few dozen start-ups turn into MNCs in the future, it can provide a significant boost to India's economic growth.

Consider the Women Entrepreneurship Platform (WEP),[23] which aims to help women realize their entrepreneurial aspirations. It is built on the premise that women often lack the information and conducive environment required to start and sustain an enterprise. WEP is an online platform that provides women entrepreneurs information about various government initiatives, knowledge about running businesses, and a community of women entrepreneurs. Through its key partnerships, WEP extends support for critical services such as funding, tax compliance assistance, marketing support, skilling, and so forth. Launched in March 2018, this is a relatively recent intervention. Still, more than 25,000 women are already registered on this platform. The programme also celebrates the stories of exceptional women that have brought about change across India and thereby creates role models for others. NITI Aayog has been giving awards since 2016 to successful Indian women entrepreneurs.

Now, consider programmes such as Mudra Yojana (2015) and Stand-Up India (2016). Both promote entrepreneurship at the grassroots level, especially among women and marginalized groups. Both Mudra Yojana and Stand-Up India offer bank loans. However, they differ in terms of the size of loan amount and intended beneficiaries: while Mudra Yojana provides loans of smaller amounts (from Rs 50,000 to Rs 10 lakh) without any collateral, Stand-Up India provides loans of higher amounts (from Rs 10 lakh to Rs 1 crore) with collateral. The former is designed to promote entrepreneurship among the lower strata of society while the latter promotes entrepreneurship among women and Scheduled Castes/Tribes. Both these programmes are designed to ensure that the benefits reach eligible people from all over the country rather than just a few regions.

Although significant amounts have been disbursed under both these programmes, Mudra Yojana is much bigger in terms of both the loans sanctioned and the number of beneficiaries. Cumulatively, over 28.7 crore loans totalling Rs 15,00,000 crore were sanctioned under Mudra Yojana, whereas nearly Rs 26,000 crore in loans were given to over 114,000 accounts under Stand-Up India.

These are new generation programmes that seek to address barriers both at an individual level and at the system level so that entrepreneurship and innovations can thrive. They are expected to create a new class of entrepreneurs and innovators who can contribute to India's growth and employment opportunities. These programmes are not cast in stone; instead, they are evolving with the changing reality.

Additionally, there are two major programmes specifically designed to address the systemic challenges of skilling India and digitalizing India.

Skilling India

The Indian labour market has been facing the twin challenges of unemployment on one hand and shortage of skilled manpower on the other. Addressing these challenges is a key development priority in a country with the world's second-largest labour force and with a sizable number of people entering the job market every year. It is hard to believe that Indian policymakers have missed addressing these issues in the past.

These issues have now received heightened attention under the Modi government and are on its list of priorities. In the first year of coming to power, the government established a separate Ministry of Skill Development and Entrepreneurship (MSDE) to coordinate all skill-development efforts. It launched Skill India Mission in 2015 to empower the youth with skillsets that would enable them to be job-ready. The mission set the foundation by creating an institutional framework to implement skill development across the country. Under this mission, the government has been implementing more than 40 skill-development schemes/programmes across 20 central ministries/departments. Since its launch, the mission has led to significant expansion of skilling infrastructure and facilities in the country. The goal of the mission was to train more than 400 million Indians in various skills by 2022. Although the mission has made a significant contribution, it has fallen short of achieving the goal by a wide margin.

India needs to intensify its efforts in skilling and re-skilling and provide recognition to informally acquired skills. Structural, demographic, and technological shifts that are underway are changing the nature of work in India as also in the world. To realize its aspiration of being the 'skill capital' of the world, it needs to work on multiple fronts such as creating pathways for international mobility and improving the low female participation in the labour force.[24]

There has been some progress in the promotion of international mobility. For instance, the Indian government facilitated internships for Indian nationals in Japan in partnership with their government. It is also collaborating with countries such as the UK, Australia, and the UAE to set mutually recognized benchmarks and standards. Government-to-government and B2B partnerships are also being developed for new markets to increase the mobility of blue- and white-collared Indian workers. Similarly, efforts are underway to develop a market-driven network to counsel and guide potential emigrants with upskilling, language, and pre-departure orientations.

The National Education Policy (NEP 2020), which has not come a day too soon, is also a serious effort to bring vocational education into mainstream education.[25] If implemented well, NEP 2020 can turn India into a global knowledge superpower, but it is a longer-term measure.

With regards to the low female participation rate, the government seems to be counting on the wider 'gender push' together with skilling initiatives to do the job, which may not be sufficient. A more proactive approach may be needed. Harnessing *naari shakti* (women power) is not just about the economic empowerment of women but also achieving higher economic growth. Greater participation of women in the labour market would drive many household activities out of the home setting and brings them into the realm of markets, thereby reinforcing the process of growth and development.

Digitalizing India

Digitalization is a powerful enabler of growth and development. Depending on its scale and spread, digitalization can further divide a society or bridge the divide. Because it cuts across the development spectrum, digitalization can vitiate or ameliorate the development divide.

The Modi government's digital goal has been to reduce both the digital and development divides. Digital India – a flagship programme of the Modi government – is aimed at creating a digitally empowered society and knowledge economy. The programme seeks to establish digital infrastructure in every nook and corner of the country and ensure that people can use it. With its launch in 2015, India has expanded its digital footprint nationwide – the programme has helped connect over 60% of gram panchayats to the internet, established a network of about 3.75 lakh self-sustaining common service centres in gram panchayats, provided mobile and internet connectivity to almost all villages, launched a scheme to make the rural population digitally literate, and so forth.

The government has taken the lead in building a strong digital foundation for India. Under Digital India, the government has developed one of the world's most robust and comprehensive digital public-good platforms, spanning Aadhar, which provides digital identities to almost 130 crore Indians, UPI (Unified Payments Interface) to make payments digitally, and the CoWin app for booking COVID vaccinations. India has successfully created over 20 public digital platforms touching a billion-plus lives in providing multiple services to citizens. Digilocker (digital depository of official documents), Umang (for providing various services, mostly digital payments or billing services), Grameen e-stores (eCommerce initiative for digital ordering and delivery), e-sanjeevni (for telemedicine), and e-NAM (connecting agricultural markets) are some of the public platforms that have been deployed at scale. These platforms are helping create a vibrant tech start-up ecosystem across different sectors. All of this is leading to enormous value creation by enabling seamless transactions, catalyzing innovation, and generating efficiency and transparency for users.

While digitalization has been one of the most important trends in India over the past few years, and the country has emerged as the second-fastest digital adopter among 17 major digital economies, there is a long way to go. It needs to continue both building digital infrastructure and ensuring that citizens can take advantage of it. For example, India needs to connect the remaining gram panchayats with the optical fibre network under the Bharatnet initiative. Similarly, it needs to intensify the digital literacy programme – Pradhan Mantri Gramin Digital Saksharta Abhiyan – to familiarize people with the use of the internet and mobile phones. Nearly four crore people (one person per rural household) have been trained and about three crore people have been tested and certified.[26] With nearly 15 crore rural households and the need to cover more members in each household, the programme has a lot more ground to cover. Furthermore, it needs to continue creating public digital platforms. With a growing dependence on digital technologies, issues such as data privacy, cyber-frauds, data localization, and so forth become exceedingly important. The government needs to invest in addressing these issues.

The government's thrust on skilling India and digitalization is consistent with its broad-based development strategy aimed at harnessing human resource potential to the fullest to drive growth.

Geographical focus

Another aspect of broad-based development concerns tapping the economic potential of different regions of the country. In the geographically diverse country that India is, each region has some uniqueness that defines and propels its local economy. Understanding and harnessing the economic potential of each region is again a part of Modi's growth strategy. The Modi government is giving special attention to the development of the north-eastern region, Jammu & Kashmir, Ladakh, Andaman & Nicobar Islands, and so forth. All of these regions are highly touristic, but to realize their trade and tourism potential, these regions need better connectivity through different means – rail, road, air, and sea. Better connectivity is needed also because of their strategic importance as these are border regions. The government is investing in several infrastructure projects to improve connectivity to these regions.

Broad-based development is also about investing in hitherto neglected regions of the country and providing opportunities to people in these regions. Their participation in the process of economic growth is essential for building a new India. The same goes for the different sectors of the economy covered in the next chapter.

Discussion

Economists are generally wary of pursuing broad-based development strategies. From an efficiency perspective, they take a grim view of such a strategy as it calls for spreading limited resources too thinly. To maximize efficiency, economies need to reap the benefits that come with agglomeration and concentration. This calls for focusing resources strategically. The Modi government's broad-based focus is seen as the opposite of this. However, a broad-based strategy may not be a bad idea from a longer-term perspective. Activating every unit that can potentially contribute to economic growth in the medium-term sounds promising, for the reasons listed as follows.

First, in a context where development is becoming an increasingly complex affair, people's engagement is an absolute necessity. Gone are the days when development entailed building a bridge or constructing a road or erecting a power plant. Once such projects were made functional, people would stand to benefit. Increasingly, economic development in India is becoming more complex. The success of development programmes requires people's active participation, whether in imparting occupational skills or improving health/educational/nutritional outcomes or resource conservation. A broad-based strategy that is people-centric serves development interests well.

Second, development challenges at the local level require local innovations that can come about only by involving local people. When development is broad-based, it becomes easier to crowdsource solutions to context-specific problems.

Third, having a broad-based strategy that is more diversified and widespread will de-risk growth, that is, make economic growth robust on a sustained basis. This strategy has a higher chance of success because even if a few dozen start-ups turn into multinationals, it can provide a significant push to India's economy. However, the small scale of most enterprises would be its downside, but this need not be worrying as long as there is demand for localized products.

Fourth, digital transformation is empowering people and giving them a voice, which can help hold authorities accountable. No government can afford to disengage its people as it charts the country's development journey. Also, technology has made it easier for governments to engage with people for monitoring and reporting any wrongdoings in public service delivery.

For all these and other reasons, the government needs to engage with the public. A broad-based development strategy makes the growth process people-centric too. It brings the masses to their feet in the pursuit of economic success. In other words, it seeks to crowdsource economic growth.

It's a different matter that broad-based development is also politically salient.

4

Growth Vistas, New and Old

The Modi government has displayed strong leadership in 'cultivating' hitherto underinvested sectors that have huge potential to boost the economy. Tourism, renewables, the blue economy (comprising ocean and coastal resources), and electric mobility are some of the sectors on which the Modi government is placing its bets. These sectors also have a significant multiplier effect – developing these sectors will have far-reaching consequences for the economy at large. Though these sectors are not new growth avenues, with many being as old as Independent India itself, they are yet to receive the policy support required for them to realize their potential.

Here are some examples of new as well as conventional sectors that the government is betting big on.

Tourism

Every country is unique in terms of its geographical, historical, and cultural attributes. As long as humans' innate desire to explore the world remains, any country that harnesses its tourism potential can secure a valuable source of income, employment, and foreign exchange.

The fact that India has plenty to offer is well-known. It is home to 40 world heritage sites, 74 percent of the Himalayas, nearly 7,500 km of coastline dotted with some of the world's most beautiful beaches, the only living desert in the world, and diverse wildlife parks. Further, it is the birthplace of four religions – Hinduism, Buddhism, Jainism, and Sikhism – and is home to many others. Given India's wealth of culture, heritage, archaeology, and biodiversity, it has huge potential for all kinds of tourism: spiritual, historic, cultural, adventure, and so forth. In other words, tourism can play a significant role in boosting the already diversified Indian economy.

Yet, this sector never got the kind of push it needed to meet its potential. Unsurprisingly, more Indian tourists travel abroad than foreign tourists come to India. In 2019, India had 24 million outbound tourists and only 11 million inbound tourists. The Modi government seeks to invert this balance.

To double the number of inbound tourists (to 20 million international tourists) by 2024, the Modi government has taken several steps: lowered taxes (reduced the GST on five-star hotel accommodation), extended concessions to the sector (e.g., tax breaks for building convention centres), reduced e-visa fees, and so forth. It has been improving connectivity to remote locations under its UDAN scheme and promoting tourism to India by advertising Indian cuisine, culture, and handicrafts.

In addition, the Modi government has been developing new tourist spots. The Statue of Unity project, located in Gujarat, is a good example. Built at a cost of nearly Rs 3,000 crore, the project makes good business sense. In its first year of operation alone, the statue attracted nearly 3 million tourists and raked in Rs. 82 crores in ticket revenue, not to mention the considerable fillip it gave to the local economy. The government has also been working on developing and promoting over 70 lighthouses to drive tourism across India's picturesque coast. The Lighthouse on Manapad beach (Tamil Nadu), Kaup beach (Karnataka), lighthouse beach (Kerala), and Jhinjhuvada town (Gujarat) are a few examples where tourism could be developed and promoted further.

Further, since 2014, India has added 10 new World Heritage Sites, which form one-fourth of our total. Recently, Dholavira – a Harrapan city in Gujarat – was added to UNESCO's World Heritage List, taking our total number to 40. This only shows the government's steadfast commitment to promoting Indian culture, heritage, and ways of life.

To improve the air connectivity of unserved and underserved areas, the government has operationalized several airports through its UDAN scheme. Under the scheme, financial incentives are extended to select airlines to encourage them to operate from underserved and unserved airports. Nearly 350 routes across the length and breadth of the country have been operationalized. Accessibility and better connectivity are key to improving tourism and economic development.

Water taxis, ROPAX ferries, and seaplanes are all part of the Modi government's strategy to improve connectivity. Though these modes of travel are not new, they have not been developed to their full potential. Soon, these will become standard modes of transport in certain areas.

India's ranking in the travel and tourism competitiveness index jumped from 65th in 2013 to 34th in 2019 as a result of these changes. This revival in India's tourism can be linked to government efforts to revive India's ancient glory by building modern infrastructure. However, tourism has been badly hit by the COVID pandemic in the following years. Though the international tourism sector is expected to recover in the long term, the government has shifted its focus inward to the revival of domestic tourism in the short term.

Similar to the 'Incredible India' campaign that was started in 2002, the Tourism Ministry launched the 'Dekho Apna Desh' campaign in January 2020. While the Incredible India campaign aimed at encouraging visitors from around the world to experience India's vast diversity, the Dekho Apna Desh campaign is aimed at promoting domestic tourism. The Incredible India campaign led to an increase in foreign visitors by 80 percent between 2002 and 2007; the Dekho Apna Desh campaign is yet to see any outcomes, largely due to the effects of the coronavirus pandemic. In due time, as more Indians explore their home country, the local economy is bound to thrive. To promote tourism in the post-COVID context, the government has been preparing a new tourism policy.

The blue economy

The Modi administration has also been working on developing the blue economy – broadly referred to as the sustainable use of ocean resources for economic growth, employment, and improved livelihoods. According to the Niti Aayog, the blue economy can serve as a growth catalyst and plays a critical role in India realizing its vision of becoming a $10 trillion economy by 2032. At present, the blue economy contributes about 4% to India's GDP, but this share has the potential to go up significantly.[27]

Some activities such as maritime trade and tourism and fishing are centuries old. However, with over 7,500 km of coastline, 14,500 potentially navigable waterways, and over 1,350 islands, India's blue economy offers huge economic potential that is yet to be exploited.

The centrepiece of India's push to develop its blue economy is the Sagarmala project launched in 2015. Improving the performance of the country's logistics sector forms the core of the undertaking. The project aims at achieving port-led development by modernizing India's ports and unlocking the potential of its waterways and coastlines. Under this highly ambitious programme, the government aims to execute nearly 400 different projects along the coastline at a whopping cost of nearly Rs 8 lakh crore over the next two decades.

Developing its waterways is important for India to bring down the high cost of logistics. India's high logistics costs are due to an inefficient modal mix, driven by a relatively inefficient road segment. While road infrastructure has massively improved over the last few years, rail and waterways need to catch up. As the dedicated rail freight network is operationalized in phases, the market share of rail is expected to increase in the modal mix. The government is also working on developing 23 waterways by 2030, as they offer a cost-effective and environment-friendly means of transport.

Cultivating a new source of economic growth is a tedious and slow process as it typically involves long processes such as framing necessary policies, building physical infrastructure, and developing regulatory mechanisms. However, once that is done, progress becomes much easier. For example, developing inland waterways requires developing reliable infrastructure – constructing jetties, establishing night navigation facilities, establishing infrastructure to maintain water levels, constructing roads to connect waterways to coastal highways, and so forth. It is also necessary to develop the required safety and communication regulations per the law.

In its 2021 monsoon session, the Parliament passed two important bills that will aid in the development of waterways. One, the Marine Aids to Navigation Bill, 2021, which seeks to provide a framework for the development, maintenance, and management of navigation aids in India. Two, the Inland Vessels Bill, 2021, which seeks to introduce a uniform regulatory framework for inland vessel navigation across the country.[28] Both these pieces of legislation will enable the development of inland waterways in the country.

Waterways, although significant, are only a part of the Sagarmala project. The project also aims to augment coastal infrastructure, intensify fishing, create special economic zones, and promote tourism. In addition, the government approved a deep ocean mission in June 2021 for the exploration of resources and is working on developing deep-sea technologies for their sustainable use. This is the first time that any government has taken a 360-degree view of our blue economy's potential.

Maritime activities fall under various sectors, such as ocean and coastal economy, energy, infrastructure, environment, shipping, law, culture, and tourism among others. Coordinating various stakeholders and integrating the activities of different sectors is crucial to realizing the blue economy's potential. Recently, the government has constituted a committee – The New Blue Economy Coordination Committee – for this very purpose.

India needs to take advantage of its blue economy potential as well as advance its security interests while maintaining an ecological balance.

Energy

India is among the countries with the lowest per-capita energy consumption. Even so, the country is heavily dependent on others for its oil and gas requirements – India meets roughly 85 percent of its oil and 54 percent of its natural gas requirements through imports. India also imports a significant share of the uranium needed for its atomic power plant.[29] There isn't much that can be done about it except to speed up the transition to cleaner energy sources (solar, wind, and green hydrogen), not only for its energy security but also for a cleaner environment and climate equity.

Like many other countries, India too is transitioning from fossil fuels (oil, gas, and coal) to cleaner energy sources. India aims to ramp up its renewable capacity to 175 GW by 2022, which it will meet in all certainty. In December 2021, India's installed renewable capacity (including large hydro) stood at 151 GW. It has set a target of installing 500 GW by 2030, which it should be able to meet at the current rate of transition.[30]

India is also positioning itself to take a leadership role in the path towards carbon neutrality. For instance, the Modi government has been the force behind the formation of the International Solar Alliance, headquartered in Delhi. The alliance consists of 102 signatory countries that lie completely or partially between the tropics of Cancer and Capricorn which aim to transition to clean energy. The alliance aims to produce one trillion watts (1000 GW) of solar energy by 2030. India is leading the way in sticking to its Paris Climate Change commitments by exponentially increasing its renewable energy capacity.

Although India is not blessed with natural resources such as oil and uranium, it is well endowed with sunshine. It gets nearly 300 days of sunshine a year. To harness this potential, the country is not only installing new solar capacity but is also introducing policies to reduce its dependence on imports of solar cells, modules, and panels from roughly 90 percent at present to 30–35 percent in the next 4–5 years. It is also working toward creating an ecosystem to support solar manufacturing and storage to enable accelerated integration of renewables into the grid (Institute for Energy Economics and Financial Analysis, July 2021).[31] Measures such as incentives for high-efficiency solar modules are being provided to boost domestic solar manufacturing and make it competitive. However, solar has its limitations too. Because it doesn't work round the clock, it needs batteries to store energy. India is currently dependent on countries such as China, Chile, Bolivia, and Australia for a critical battery ingredient – lithium.

India is also working on making greater use of affordable biofuels, providing an alternate source of income to farmers,[32] and reducing India's import dependence. India is currently mixing 9 percent of biofuel with petrol (up from less than 2 percent in 2014) and has a target of raising this to 20 percent by 2025.[33] It is also attempting to leverage the potential of other local sources of energy such as biomass.

To diversify its energy mix, India is serious about developing green hydrogen as one of its options and, accordingly, it launched the National Green Hydrogen Mission in August 2021 to build a hydrogen ecosystem. Hydrogen is the most abundant element on the planet but rarely in its pure form. Its energy density is almost three times that of diesel, which makes it a rich source of energy. Hydrogen fuel is made through electrolysis, where energy is used to split water into hydrogen and oxygen. When the energy used in this process comes from renewables such as wind and solar, the hydrogen fuel so made is called green hydrogen.[34] Green hydrogen is a zero-carbon fuel.

However, the challenge with green hydrogen is twofold: one, sourcing the immense amount of renewable energy required to compress or liquefy it, and two, storing it at a stable temperature of minus 253 °C before use, which makes it very costly. Its production cost (much of which comes from electricity costs) is the main obstacle.

According to some estimates, this cost is expected to come down for nations having perpetual sunshine and vast unused land.[35] As India is a geographically diverse country, acquiring land in areas with high sunshine and developing adequate transmission and distribution infrastructure to connect solar farms to industrial centres will be key. Once this has been done, scaling up the production of green hydrogen will help make it more affordable. Surplus electricity from renewable energy sources can completely change the economics of green hydrogen production.

This green hydrogen can be used to generate power or in other industries. For example, it is used in the production of ammonia (currently being imported) used in fertilizers, in the mobility sector, and in refining petroleum (that is, segregating diesel and petrol). It can also be used in the steel, cement, glass, and other industries.[36] It can also be blended with compressed natural gas and supplied as piped fuel. For these reasons, it is dubbed as the fuel of the future.

When coal is used in the production of hydrogen, it's called brown hydrogen. As India is well endowed with coal, the government is keen to produce hydrogen using coal. Accordingly, the government has constituted a task force and expert committee to prepare a roadmap for coal-based hydrogen production.[37] Despite India's best efforts to adopt clean energy sources, its dependence on fossil fuels is only going to increase in the future. As India moves towards achieving higher economic prosperity, it will need more energy. However, India's current energy mix is heavily dependent on thermal power. Of the total capacity of 393 GW as on December 2021, nearly 235 GW comes from thermal.[38] India will need to invest strategically to reduce its dependence on thermal sources and transition to renewables.

In addition to producing more energy, India will need to put it to more efficient uses as well. The government's Saksham programme aims to sensitize the public about clean fuel choices and the need for energy conservation. It intends to educate them of the benefits of green energy for individuals, families, communities, and the country as a whole and make them stakeholders in the green energy transition.

Energy conservation needs to become a national habit through the promotion of renewables wherever possible. E.g., using solar for irrigation, installing fuel-efficient gadgets (e.g., LED blubs), using public transport as well as bicycles wherever and whenever possible, and so forth. These changes will not only help reduce costs but also aid in ensuring cleaner air.

The government has set a goal of making India energy-independent before 2047 when the country completes 100 years of independence.

Electric mobility

In the fight against climate change, electric mobility, particularly electric vehicle (EV) technologies, are key.

The Modi government's policy support for electric vehicles was motivated by the twin objectives of addressing environmental pollution and fuel security.[39] In 2015, the government launched the FAME India scheme for the Faster Adoption and Manufacturing of Electric and Hybrid Vehicles. Under the scheme, the government offered incentives to subsidize the cost of EVs and promote the establishment of charging infrastructure. In 2019, the government launched the second phase of FAME, focused mainly on incentivizing demand by offering subsidies for the electrification of public and shared transportation (e-buses, e-3 wheelers, e-4 wheeler passenger cars, and e-2 wheelers).[40]

The government is now speeding up the transition to EVs to provide a boost to the automobile industry.[41] The government is offering Production Linked Incentives (PLIs) of Rs 26,000 crore for the automobile sector (including drones) to trigger the transition to newer technologies. It is estimated that the PLI scheme will attract Rs 42,500 crore of fresh investment into the automotive industry, spur incremental production of over Rs. 2.3 lakh crore, and help create more than 7.5 lakh jobs over this period.[42] It is expected to herald a new age of automotive manufacturing. Subsequently, MSMEs in the auto component sector too will get a boost.[43] The creation of an entire ecosystem around EVs, including the circular economy,[44] will boost economic growth. The government plans to have at least 30 percent of private cars, 70 percent of commercial vehicles, 40 percent of buses, and 80 percent of two- and three-wheelers shift to electric by 2030.

Charging infrastructure, which is essential for a smooth transition to electric mobility, is being rapidly constructed. The government has issued guidance for states and local bodies to frame policies and norms for setting up charging networks.[45] To boost demand for EVs, the government has come out with a national scrappage policy and is offering several incentives such as tax concessions. Additionally, it has started a 'Go Electric' campaign to spread awareness about the benefits of EVs and encourage the public to switch from combustion vehicles to EVs. State governments too have started coming up with EV policies and provide additional incentives. Odisha and Gujarat are among the states that have taken the lead.

Undoubtedly, India's transition to EVs is better for the country as a whole for several reasons: reduced vehicular emissions will lower air pollution and ensure cleaner air in cities,[46] higher economic growth due to technological disruption in the automotive sector, a faster transition to new technologies in the mobility space, reduced risk of road accidents with safer technologies, growth of the circular economy, higher tax revenues for the government, etc. From the user's perspective too, the transition to EVs brings some distinct benefits: improved mobility experience, low maintenance and operational costs, health benefits from reduced pollution, and so forth. Even so, a policy of compulsory scrapping of overaged vehicles may impose huge costs on some users. This remains true regardless of how scientific the process to weed out unfit vehicles is.

Besides EVs, the government is also trying to make it mandatory for auto manufacturers to offer flex-fuel vehicles (FFVs) that can run 100 percent on bio-fuels (ethanol/methanol). FFVs help in cutting down emissions and reducing India's petroleum import bill. The government is also encouraging the development of hydrogen technologies for the mobility sector.

India may have missed the first-mover advantage in making the lithium-ion batteries that are essential for EVs. Nevertheless, it still has the potential to become a leader in the EV space as it is exploring alternatives to lithium-ore batteries such as aluminium-ion batteries and sodium-ion batteries.

Developments in the EV space represent innovations in existing modes of transportation.[47] Equally, the government is promoting innovative modes through drones, etc. Thus, India is straddling both, conventional and modern transportation systems.

Modi is truly visionary with his short-term as well as longer-term targets. India has never had the kind of leadership required to take its economy anywhere close to its potential. Over the years, the onslaught of imported goods has destroyed its small and medium scale industries across sectors, be it toys, bicycles, stationery products, shoes, or clocks. The Indian government could have done a lot to retain the competitiveness of its domestic industry, but measures needed to put up a strong defence in the face of the fierce foreign competition have been absent. As a result, India let several of its MSMEs meet a slow death. Indian manufacturers turned into importers and traders. Some manufacturers set up manufacturing units in China and shipped their products for sale to India, which had limited beneficial effects. The Modi government is trying to correct some of these problems.

Traditional growth drivers

The government has also been strengthening traditional growth drivers. Three such drivers considered here are agriculture, MSMEs, and infrastructure.

Agriculture is considered the backbone of the Indian economy for the food it provides, its interaction with the industry, and for the size of the labour force it engages, including womenfolk. Agriculture must do well if the Indian economy is to prosper. The Modi government has rightly been emphasizing agriculture from the beginning and set an ambitious goal of doubling farmers' incomes by 2023.[48]

The problems with Indian agriculture are multi-fold. One, over 85 percent of farmers are marginal farmers with small landholdings – this results in low farm productivity, weak bargaining power, and hence, low farmer incomes. To overcome these challenges, aggregation of farm holdings is a must.

Two, irrational use of agricultural inputs – mainly water, electricity, and fertilizers – is another big challenge. For example, 75 to 80 percent of irrigated water goes to just three crops (rice, wheat, and sugarcane). Crop diversification is necessary to overcome this and the associated challenges of introducing more sustainable and climate-resilient agriculture.

Third, farmers do very little value addition to their agricultural produce. This is one of the major reasons why farmers don't get remunerative prices for their produce. Lack of processing of agricultural produce also contributes to its wastage. This challenge can be addressed through higher unit value realization with greater agro-processing.

The Modi government has attempted to come up with a comprehensive strategy to deal with various challenges facing Indian agriculture and farmers. For example, the government has introduced the e-NAM platform – an online transparent bidding system – for better market linkage. This has enhanced farmers' access to multiple markets and buyers and has thereby helped farmers transparently realize remunerative prices. Already 1,000 markets across 18 states and three union territories have been integrated. So far, more than 1.69 crore farmers and 1.55 lakh traders are registered on the e-NAM platform. The intent is to have 'One Nation, One Market' for agricultural produce.

Similarly, the government is promoting farmer producer organizations (FPOs) in a big way. By forming farmers' collectives, small farmers can realize some advantages of scale in terms of reduced input costs, higher prices for their produce, and improved access to technology. Anywhere between 4,000 to 5,000 FPOs currently exist. The government has been trying to raise this number to 10,000 and create a revolution in food processing. It is aspiring to increase the export of processed food to 400 billion dollars in the coming years. It has also deepened ongoing interventions for providing irrigation and electricity facilities, financially protecting farmers in the event of crop failure due to various natural calamities, providing institutional credit to farmers, ensuring rational use of fertilizers through neem coating of urea, and, more recently, through use of nano-urea and so forth.

Micro, small and medium enterprises (MSMEs)

The government has been giving special emphasis to the MSME sector, which is the second-most important sector in terms of employment, following agriculture. MSMEs are important also because they contribute 30 percent of India's GDP and 48 percent of exports. The government is aiming to increase the sector's contribution to 40 percent of the GDP, as it considers it critical to realizing its overarching $5 trillion goal.

The Modi government has introduced a slew of measures to promote and develop the MSME sector. For example, it has initiated the MSME cluster development programme, established a credit guarantee fund for MSMEs, and instituted a credit-linked capital subsidy for technology upgradation.

The government is giving preference to micro and small enterprises in the public procurement of commodities by reserving 25 percent of procurement by central government or public-sector enterprises for such enterprises. Likewise, it has reserved 358 items for exclusive procurement from micro and small enterprises. It has brought retail and wholesale trade under the ambit of MSMEs. This measure will enable retail and wholesale traders to avail the benefits of priority-sector lending under the RBI guidelines. This decision will potentially benefit 2.5 crore retail and wholesale traders.

It has not only revised the criteria for the classification of MSMEs but has also developed a new process of MSME registration – Udyam Registration. Also, it has developed an online portal called Champions, which covers many aspects of e-governance including grievance redressal and providing guidance for MSMEs.

All this shows the government's commitment to strengthening the MSME sector and turning it into a growth engine.

Infrastructure

The Modi government has been giving special attention to building next-generation infrastructure with the view of improving both ease of living and doing business. Towards this end, it has launched/intensified work on several schemes including Bharatmala (2017), Sagarmala (2015), Dedicated Freight Corridor (2006), UDAN (2016), and inland waterways. The pace of infrastructure development under the Modi government is truly unprecedented, whether it is in the construction of national highways, enhancing regional air connectivity, improving rail connectivity to the North-East region, increasing the capacity of major ports, etc.

Recently, the Modi government launched Gati Shakti, a digital platform that facilitates integrated planning and coordinated implementation of infrastructure connectivity projects by bringing together several ministries. This would enable the government to strategize better and further speed up infrastructure development. Also, it will provide vital information to investors, the business community, and the public at large so that they can sync their activities with the government's infrastructure development plan.

These are then just a few sectors, both new and old, where we see the Modi government's approach to growth and development. Although significant progress has been made in each of these sectors, a lot remains to be done to realize India's true economic potential.

5

Tiny Tweaks

Even as the government has been focused on enacting some big-ticket, politically-contentious reforms, it has not shied away from making smaller tweaks that can contribute to India's growth story. Here are a few examples that demonstrate this in action.

The bamboo conflict

According to the Indian Forest Act,[49] bamboo was defined as a tree – this classification made the resource inaccessible to communities that were directly dependent on bamboo for their livelihoods. Also, it acted as a major impediment for bamboo cultivation by farmers on non-forest land. To permit cultivation, felling, and transit of bamboo grown in non-forest areas, the Modi government promulgated the Indian Forest (Amendment) Ordinance in 2017, classifying non-forest bamboo as a grass. The stated objective of this amendment was two-fold: one, to improve the earnings of tribals and communities living around forests; and two, to increase the green cover of the country.

With the Parliament passing this amendment, bamboo in non-forest areas could be freely produced and transported. Those dependent on bamboo for their livelihoods could now access more market opportunities. Bamboo wood is in high demand as it is used extensively in a variety of applications such as the production of furnishing, yarn, pulp and paper, handicrafts, decoration, and musical instruments.

Neem-coated urea

When the Modi government assumed power, a policy already existed mandating the production of a certain percentage of subsidized urea. The Fertilizer Control Order was passed in 1957 by the Government of India to regulate the pricing and sales of urea. However, in 2015, the Modi government made it mandatory to produce 100% of subsidized urea as neem-coated. This policy was applicable to imported urea as well, which was coated with neem oil in ports.[50]

In India, urea is used as a fertilizer to add nitrogen to the soil. As it is highly soluble in water, nitrification and de-nitrification reduce its efficiency. If urea is coated with neem, the loss can be minimized, as the coating slows down the release of fertilizer, which then remains available to plants for a longer duration. Coating urea with neem is environmentally friendly in multiple ways: it reduces the solubility of urea, thus reducing groundwater contamination; reduces ammonia volatilization; and controls atmospheric pollution. Moreover, the increased efficiency of the fertilizer is economically beneficial to farmers.[51] The beneficial effects of neem-coated urea were known as early as the 1970s. However, controls on the selling price of urea discouraged commercial production of neem-coated urea. It was not until 2008 that the government allowed urea manufacturers to recover the costs of coating from farmers. Still, the government capped the production of neem-coated urea in relation to total production. This cap was gradually eased over time. It turns out that even neem-coated urea may get displaced over time as better alternates become available.

Recent advances have led to the development of nano urea, which is a better alternative to conventional urea that is applied to soil. The Indian Farmers Fertilizer Cooperative (IFFCO) has developed a nanotechnology-based nano urea (liquid) fertilizer that overcomes the problems associated with the use of conventional urea. It is a home-grown innovation developed for the first time in the world. Field trials of nano urea have demonstrated it to be economical and effective as it results in higher crop yield, is safe for humans, and is environment friendly.[52] The government is mulling over how to encourage the balanced use of nano urea.

Increasing the retirement age of government doctors

That India has an acute shortage of doctors is a well-known fact. This shortage didn't emerge overnight but is the result of a lack of political will. The Medical Council of India (MCI), which regulated Medical Education and Medical Practices in India, was a major stumbling block. MCI was run by a corrupt cabal that had many influential politicians in its pocket.[53] Many people attributed the shortage of doctors in the country to the failure of MCI in discharging its core responsibilities. Scrapping the MCI and replacing it with another body was probably the only way to deal with the problem. The UPA government tried doing so but was unsuccessful, perhaps due to the reality of coalition politics. This was finally accomplished by the Modi government immediately after coming to power in the second term. A bill relating to the National Medical Commission – which was to replace the MCI – aimed at reforming medical education to meet the widening demand for healthcare workers was passed in August 2019.

While this much-needed reform was still in the making, the government took a short-term measure in the interim. It increased the retirement age of doctors in central health services to 65 years with effect from 31 May, 2016, which benefitted about 4,000 central government doctors. The idea was to retain experienced doctors for a longer period so that they could continue providing quality health services to citizens, particularly the poor.

However, most doctors don't really 'retire'. Post-superannuation, they continue working as demand for their services is high. They either find lucrative opportunities in the private sector or start their own practices after retirement. So, the real strength of this policy tweak is unknown, but it didn't stop the government from doing it anyway.

Maitri Setu bridge (2021)

Here is an example from infrastructure which shows how the Modi government isn't afraid of undertaking projects that are small but important. A small investment running in a few hundred crores of rupees means nothing in a sector that is known to be an investment guzzler. Maitri Setu bridge over the Feni river – which flows along the Indian boundary between Tripura and Bangladesh – is one such project.

Maitri Setu is a 1.9 km bridge entailing an investment of nearly Rs 133 crores. Yet, this bridge is important as it is expected to boost the production of various bamboo products and also increase the pineapple and agarbatti (incense sticks) business in Agartala. With improved connectivity, it is expected to strengthen economic activities in both countries. The bridge joins Sabroom in India with Ramgarh in Bangladesh.

A World Bank report on the challenges and opportunities of transport integration in Eastern South Asia states that seamless transport connectivity between the two has the potential to increase the national income of Bangladesh by 17 percent and India by 8 percent.[54] Maitri Setu is a small step in this direction.

According to the analysis, a free trade agreement between India and Bangladesh together with improved transport connectivity between them could increase India's export to Bangladesh by 172 percent while Bangladesh's export to India could rise by almost 297 percent.

National Handloom Day

At a time when trade in man-made fibre and technical textiles is on the rise, khadi and handloom products seem a little out of place. In India, however, handloom textiles are not just a symbol of its glorious cultural heritage but also an important source of livelihood for a large number of people. With over 70 percent of handloom weavers and allied workers being women, it is key to women empowerment too.

To generate awareness about the importance of the handloom industry and its role in India's socio-economic development, the Government of India in 2015 declared August 7 as National Handloom Day. Why August 7th? It is because, on this day in 1905, the Swadeshi Movement was launched in Calcutta Town Hall to protest the partition of Bengal by the British government. Just like the Swadeshi Movement, this initiative aims to revive domestic products and production processes.

In the past, PM Modi has promoted the use of khadi in everyday life and sought to position the purchase of khadi as a service to the people and the nation. On the eve of Mahatma Gandhi's birthday, he urged citizens to buy khadi to offer tribute to the father of the nation.

If people were to start using khadi products in large quantities, it could mean a lot to those whose livelihoods depend on khadi.

To double handloom production and quadruple its exports in the next three years, the government constituted a committee to suggest ways to upend the game.[55] Though it is a relatively small sector, this hasn't deterred the government from prioritizing it.

For most politicians, these are fleeting issues. They deal with them ritualistically. Here today and gone tomorrow. PM Modi has been steadfast in promoting this because he believes in it with deep conviction.

Jan Aushadhi Yojana

It is a well-known fact that much of healthcare expenditure in India is borne by people at the time of illness. This constitutes a huge financial burden on households. Much of this spending goes towards the purchase of drugs and diagnostics. To address this, the UPA government started an initiative in 2008 to make quality generic drugs available at affordable prices through dedicated stores. Although important, it remained a fledgling intervention under the UPA government.

At a time when the Modi government is undertaking major changes in the health sector,[56] this intervention may be easily forgotten or kept aside... but not quite! The Modi government fine-tuned the intervention and scaled it up. There are currently 8,336 Janaushadhi stores across 736 districts. The government has set a target of increasing the number of Pradhan Mantri Bhartiya Janaushadhi Kendras to 10,000 by March 2024. As per the government, the medicines available under PMBJP are priced 50 percent to 90 percent lesser than that of branded medicines. These stores have helped people (mostly low- and middle-income households) save around Rs. 4,000 crores in 2020–21.[57]

Promoting Sowa-Rigpa – Indigenous Tibetan medicine

Over the years, alternate systems of medicine (AYUSH) have not received the attention they deserve. As a result, allopathy has come to dominate the scene, even for minor ailments for which AYUSH is known to be quite effective.

While the Modi government has been promoting AYUSH in general, it has been giving due importance to the indigenous Tibetan medicine system known as Sowa-Rigpa. Although the government recognized Sowa-Rigpa in 2009, it was least promoted within AYUSH. Sowa-Rigpa is one of the oldest and most well-documented medicine systems practised widely in the Himalayan Region, outside of which not many people even know about it. There are around 1,000 practitioners of Sowa-Rigpa in India – who mostly reside in the Himalayan regions, with Dharamshala and Ladakh being the main centres.

Most herbs used in Sowa-Rigpa are grown in the Trans-Himalayan region, particularly Ladakh, which is known for its herbal wealth. The National Research Institute for Sowa-Rigpa has found 1,000 species of herbs in Ladakh. Out of these, 525 species have been identified as either medicinal or having aromatic value. The Ladakh administration is taking several measures to preserve herbs from extinction and is ramping up the R&D on the herbal wealth of the region. The administration is in the process of establishing a State Medicinal Plants Board for the promotion of medicinal plants in Ladakh.

Fit India Movement

In addition to starting Khelo India – a national programme for the development of sports and promotion of yoga – the Modi government started the Fit India movement. The Fit India movement aims to encourage people to live healthier lifestyles by spreading awareness, encouraging indigenous sports, and creating a platform for people to share their stories. Whatever little expenses incurred under the mission are borne directly by the concerned ministry – the Ministry of Youth Affairs and Sports. While the government must be spending only a tiny amount on this mission, its significance is huge.

To conclude, these are but a few examples of tiny tweaks that were not overlooked or forgotten in the wider canvas of development by the Modi government. Some other examples include getting a GI (geographical indications) tag for India's agricultural products, finding new markets for Indian fruits to diversify India's export basket of primary commodities, passing legislations banning e-cigarettes and commercial surrogacy in the country, developing remote geographies (e.g., Ladakh), or paying special attention to neglected sections of the society (e.g., the tribals). Examples of small tweaks range from running advocacy campaigns to the framing of policies to designing and implementing small but significant programmes. This only highlights the Modi government's commitment to development for all.

6

Push for Atmanirbhar Bharat

Quite early on in the COVID crisis, the Modi government launched the Atmanirbhar Bharat Abhiyaan (ANBA) or the Self-reliant India campaign to tap into India's potential for growth and development.

The Modi government's vision for new India fits perfectly with ANBA. In a televised address to the nation on May 12, 2020, Modi presented his vision and announced a special economic package of around Rs. 20 lakh crore – 10% of the country's GDP – to fight the COVID pandemic in India. The contents of this package (ANB 1.0) were subsequently announced by the finance minister in five tranches, following which the government announced two more ANB packages (ANB 2.0 and ANB 3.0). However, before addressing the details of ANBA, here is a preview of its broad outlook.

ANB 1.0 was intended to help workers, farmers, street vendors, tribals, and industries including MSMEs cope with the hardships resulting from the coronavirus pandemic. It aimed to provide relief to certain sections of society by increasing liquidity and ensuring the flow of credit to loan-seeking companies. It was less of an economic stimulus, meant to sustain rather than jumpstart the economy.

Thereafter, the government announced two more packages (ANB 2.0 and ANB 3.0). The second package (ANB 2.0) was aimed largely at boosting economic demand by raising the capital expenditure of central and state governments and introducing a leave travel concession cash voucher scheme. In the government's reckoning, these measures were expected to boost demand by more than Rs 1 lakh crore.

The third package (ANB 3.0) was designed to provide economic stimulus. While this package consisted of several measures, nearly two-thirds of the total package amount was allocated to the Production Linked Incentive Scheme (PLIs) to encourage investments and production in the manufacturing sector. The government also undertook a slew of economic reforms and policy changes such as the redefinition of MSMEs, commercialization of the mineral sector, agriculture and labour reforms, privatization of public sector undertakings, and so forth.

However, the contents of the ANBA packages are not entirely compatible with the term 'Atmanirbhar Bharat' or 'Self-reliant India'. For example, the PM – Street Vendor's Atma Nirbhar Nidhi (PM SVANidhi) Scheme may have been an important pillar of support for street vendors during the coronavirus pandemic, but it is in no way connected to creating a self-reliant India. Another example is the 'One Nation One Card' initiative, which enables migrant workers and their families to buy subsidized rations from any fair price shop anywhere in the country. Despite having been helpful to many, how does the scheme contribute to a self-reliant India?

In the government's conception of ANBA, it absolutely does. The stated goal of ANBA is to make the country and its citizens independent and self-reliant in all senses.[58] The idea of making the country self-reliant is very different from the idea of making every citizen independent and self-reliant. These ideas need to be unpacked for us to understand them better. The five pillars of Atma Nirbhar Bharat – economy, infrastructure, system, demography, and demand – are so broad that every past, present, and future economic decision taken by the government under these pillars can now be seen through the lens of ANBA.

While it has become an umbrella term for most of the government's work, there isn't a good understanding as to what constitutes ANB, and this has been the source of quite some debate.

The confusing narrative around ANB

There are several reasons the narrative attached to ANB is confusing. For one, the government has prefixed the term '*Atma Nirbhar*' to phrases such as '*Atma Nirbhar Kisan*' (self-reliant farmer), '*Atma Nirbhar Gram*' (self-reliant village), '*Atma Nirbhar Krishi*' (self-reliant agriculture), and so forth. The term finds mention even in India's victories in sports! While addressing the eighteenth convocation of Tezpur University (Assam) in January 2021, Modi is reported to have said that the spirit of ANB pervades everyday life – from cricket field to covid fight. Nationalistic sentiments may have played a role in bringing out the best among players in a highly competitive sport like cricket, but linking the sport to ANB seems a little far-fetched. Lately, self-reliance is even being associated with the concept of self-confidence!

Another confusing aspect of the narrative is that it is being attached to the philosophical concept of Vasudhaiva Kutumbakam – the world is one family. This concept was alluded to by PM Modi in his address to the nation on 12th May 2020 when he first announced ANBA.[59] Similarly, Srimad Bhagavadgita's teachings of selflessness in serving the world and its people may be globally recognized and practised, but calling India's chosen development path of ANB as consistent with Gita's mantra is not very helpful.[60]

To give another example, addressing the sixteenth Pravasi Bharatiya Divas convention in January 2021, President Ram Nath Kovind said that an Atmanirbhar Bharat would better the world order by promoting greater cooperation and peace.[61] The connection between ANB and such philosophical underpinnings is far from obvious and leaves a lot to the imagination. Even the Dalai Lama seems to have joined the bandwagon. Greeting PM Modi on his seventy-first birthday, the Dalai Lama mentioned in his letter that India's success would benefit not only the people of India but also contribute to the development of the world as a whole.[62] India's achievements may well be beneficial for the country and also globally.[63]

Unsurprisingly then, the concept has led to some confusion and has evoked sharp reactions among certain sections.

What is ANB?

The essence of ANB is not complete self-reliance but making India competitive and forging stronger economic ties with the world. It includes themes such as self-sufficiency, greater self-reliance, 'Make-in-India', 'Vocal for Local', and 'Local for Global'. India is aspiring to become self-sufficient in the production of commodities such as palm oil, rock phosphate (a key ingredient in the production of fertilizer), and the like. Other areas where it is trying to become more (and not completely) self-reliant include toy production, renewable energy generation, defence manufacturing, and so forth. It is also aspiring to play a bigger role in the global supply chain. ANB is a much stronger version of the Make-in-India campaign, which was started by the Modi government within months of coming to power in 2014.

Make-in-India

Under the Make-in-India campaign, the government has been promoting India as a preferred global manufacturing destination. The objective is to raise the share of manufacturing in GDP from 15 percent to 25 percent and create 100 million jobs in a few years. This is expected to boost economic growth, employment, and exports. The campaign promised four key changes: improving business environments, constructing modern infrastructure, adding new sectors (identified 25 sectors in manufacturing, infrastructure, and service industries), and bringing about a change in the government's interface with the industry. To promote Make-in-India and attract private investments (both domestic and foreign), the Modi government has – over the years – pursued several economic reforms. It has also taken several measures to remove the obstacles that make India uncompetitive. For example, it has provided support for infrastructure development and significantly reduced compliance burdens. Still, significant scope exists for doing more, especially at the state level.

ANBA is more potent than Make-in-India as it offers financial incentives to firms to become global champions in select areas of manufacturing. It seeks to achieve this through production-linked incentives (PLIs) for incremental investments and sales from products manufactured in India. In March 2020, the government approved the PLI scheme for three product areas: large-scale electronics, pharma ingredients/inputs, and medical devices. In November 2020, ten additional product areas were brought under the PLI programme. The government plans to allocate Rs. 1.97 lakh crore for the PLIs schemes across 13 key sectors over the next five years. The scheme is expected to result in increased output of $500 billion in five years.

The biggest chunk of incentives is for automobile and auto component companies (Rs. 57,000 crore), electronics and components (Rs. 51,000 crore), and pharmaceuticals and active pharmaceutical ingredients (Rs. 15,000 crore). In due time, the government may offer PLIs in a few more sectors – for instance, developing an entire ecosystem for semiconductors and display manufacturing in India. This goes to show that the PLI scheme is quite dynamic.

Through this scheme, the government seeks to make Indian manufacturers globally competitive, attract investments in the areas of core competency and cutting-edge technologies, ensure efficiencies, create economies of scale, enhance exports, and make India an integral part of the global supply chain. PLIs set in place a virtuous cycle of investments, employment, production, and development in the regions in which the concerned companies are located.

Vocal for Local

'Vocal for Local' is aimed at influencing the demand side – Indians – to buy local products and be more vocal in their promotion of local products. PM Modi even urged Indians to analyse their products and find ways to generate their production within the country. Since the launch of this idea in May 2020, he has mentioned the concept in every episode of his monthly radio programme, Mann ki Baat, urging citizens to adopt locally sourced products.

The idea isn't confined only to products. It extends also to promoting domestic breeds of animals such as dogs and cows.[64] Every time PM Modi has urged people to take action in the larger interest of the nation, it has had a positive effect. It should surprise no one then to find an increased demand for 'Made-in-India' products a few years down the line. Anti-Chinese sentiments are prevalent for several reasons such as China's alleged role in fuelling the Coronavirus pandemic and the recent India–China border dispute may also intensify this process.

Vocal for Local is also about promoting India-specific standards – such as developing indigenous footwear sizing standards – for which a large survey is already underway. To date, India has been following either English or US standards in footwear manufacturing.

Local Goes Global

While the previous campaign was aimed at all Indians, the Local for Global campaign is directed particularly at non-resident Indians (NRIs), students, and the youth. It revolves around building up the brand of India. PM Modi believes that the increased use of Indian products by these subgroups can encourage their use globally.

Students and youth play an important role in developing new and innovative solutions to scale local products to an international level. Achieving global recognition of brand India is a 'collective' responsibility. An important prerequisite for strengthening the brand is producing quality products and building up the credibility of Indian products.

The government is working closely with the manufacturing industry to ensure that Indian products meet global standards. In fact, the PLI scheme is already operational. The government now needs to provide conducive conditions to ensure that the companies that have applied for PLIs meet their targets.

Work towards transforming India into a global manufacturing hub has already commenced. The government has undertaken a host of economic reforms, including relaxation in FDI limits, to attract domestic and foreign investments. India is building new capabilities in specific areas. In the defence sector, for example, India is continuously growing its capacity to indigenously design, develop, and manufacture advanced cutting-edge technologies and systems.[65] ANBA will contribute to India achieving the goal of turning into a $5 trillion economy by 2025.

How does the world view ANB?

Given India's growth potential, most major countries have been trying to contribute to – as well as benefit from – India's growth story. However, ANB has created some fear and consternation among India's trading partners. Dealing with the economic crisis wreaked by a once-in-a-century pandemic requires special measures, and having a belligerent neighbour inclined to create disturbances along the border in Ladakh justifies the use of trade restrictions. An extraordinary situation does require extraordinary measures.

However, the continuation and intensification of ANB haven't gone down well among trading partners. ANB and Vocal for Local are viewed as economic nationalism. Increasing import tariffs are cited as an example of protectionism, which foreign nations believe could be counterproductive. In their view, India should be attracting investors due to its strengths rather than using tariffs to push international businesses to invest in India. They view ANBA as being an import-substituting policy that acts as a significant trade barrier. Is this true?

According to the Government of India, it is not. In its view, the self-reliant India programme is about integrating the Indian economy with the global economy as it seeks to play a greater role in global supply chains. It is capitalizing on post-COVID 'China Plus One' sentiments as companies look to diversify their supply chains.[66] India has the capacity, capability, and reliability to strengthen global supply chains and emerge as a trusted supply chain partner and manufacturing hub.

Over the last few years, the government has moved some consumer items (e.g., air conditioners, tyres, television sets) to the prohibited list and beefed-up import duties. This is partly to curb cheap imports – mostly from China – and partly to build domestic manufacturing capability. These measures seek to substitute imports with domestic production in select products.

Alongside selective protectionism, India has been pursuing a series of economic reforms to boost investments – both domestic and foreign – in the manufacturing space. Under the ANB campaign, India has opened several sectors to foreign investors including defence, atomic energy, agriculture, insurance, healthcare, and civil aviation. Further, India has continuously been taking steps to improve ease of business to make the country more attractive to investors.

India has also been tweaking its relatively-high tariff structures as it has started looking at the issue of global trade through the scope of value chains. While levying higher duties on imports of final products, India has been lowering duties on inputs. This is being done for select products where India has a major market. This could encourage companies to aggressively shift some part of their value chain to India. India's massive consumer base will drive the growth of these companies as well as the global economy. Thus, India is looking to forge greater trade and investment ties with other countries and not less, as feared by some trading partners.

It is to be noted that some of the concerns of the trading partners have nothing to do with ANB. Those concerns are either long-standing or new in emerging domains. For example, the US has been trying to gain access to India's dairy market for some time now, for which India is willing – provided the products are certified to have been derived from a dairy cow that has been fed a vegetarian diet its entire life. India defends its position on religious and cultural grounds. Similarly, weak protection and enforcement of intellectual property rights in India has been a long-standing concern that the US has with India. These are not new concerns but may have become stronger now that India is pursuing ANBA. However, these concerns will likely get sorted out with progressive talks between the two sides. Some other emerging areas of concern are norms associated with data localization and data privacy, which are a part of the larger issue of digital sovereignty. A clash between international law and national sovereignty is quite natural, not just for India but for many other countries. Whether this issue needs to be sorted out within trade agreements or outside of it is a moot point. These are all genuine but ongoing concerns and not specifically the results of ANB.

These concerns notwithstanding, significant scope exists for India to evolve its trade policy that is coherent and consistent with its objective of greater integration with global value chains.[67]

Discussion

The debate around ANB has two major segments: PLIs and pursuing import substitution as implied in the strategy.

Some experts are critical of the PLIs despite the merit of its design. PLI is a non-tariff measure that promotes manufacturing at home while encouraging investments from within and abroad. It is simple, easy to implement, and targets specific product areas. Because the quantum of subsidies is not specifically linked to either exports or local value addition, it complies with the rules of the World Trading Organization. Also, PLI is superior to other incentives, such as tax or credit, which can be problematic.[68] Yet, some economists are critical of the scheme as it relates to firm-level incentives, which they believe are difficult to monitor.[69] Instead, they favour system-level incentives to offset the high cost of production in general or to actively support specific industries (instead of firms). Still, others believe in using levers such as exchange rates rather than PLIs to boost exports.[70] Hence, even for a thoughtfully designed PLI scheme, critics do exist.

Many see ANB as an import-substitution strategy, where imports are progressively replaced through domestic production. Based on this interpretation, trade economists are critical of it and claim that it is doomed to fail. Global evidence suggests that import substitution strategies that became popular in the 1960s eventually fell out of favour in the 1990s due to the emergence of the Washington Consensus, which supported free trade.[71] History tells us that an import substitution strategy creates inefficient domestic industries propped up by favourable tariffs. Such a strategy stifles exports and deprives a country of much-needed foreign exchange. In contrast, outward-oriented or export-promotion strategies have the opposite effect – it forces the domestic industry to become competitive and produce for the global market. As per the critics, India's own experience bears testimony to the benefits of freer trade. Indeed, India's average growth rate increased post-1991, when it moved away from protectionist policies to embrace freer trade.[72]

However, it isn't difficult to see the logic behind ANBA, and those who designed the scheme are not oblivious of India's history. ANBA is neither a full-blown import-substitution strategy nor is the current context the same as back then. ANBA is import substitution in selective areas where India has the potential to emerge as a global player. The conditions that made the cost structure high for domestic manufacturing are changing, and India today is much more open to trade and investment than it has ever been.

The much-cited example of healthcare commodities (e.g., face masks and personal protection kits) – in which India not only become self-sufficient but also started exporting to other countries – may not be entirely representative, but it did show the way on how India could turn the situation to its advantage. India is now capitalizing on similar potential in selected areas.

Trade economists who see ANB from the lens of conventional trade theories are missing out on a unique economic reality that requires an innovative response. In the COVID context, as a result of disruptions in supply chains, demand for certain commodities have shot up, businesses are discovering improved methods, and entrepreneurs have found new risk-taking appetites. It's time to step back and review India's economic potential, identify promising areas, and go all out investing in building new capacities and capabilities. It's time to take advantage of India's huge domestic market, achieve the scale needed to lower costs, and become globally competitive. It's time to build comparative advantages in newer areas. Finally, at a time when several countries (US and China included) are taking steps to re-shore domestic manufacturing, India's ANBA is not out of place. India's trade policy needs to be seen as embedded in its larger strategic response to the changing geopolitical context.

Whether and to what extent ANBA serves India's economic interests remains to be seen. Who is proved right, the trade economists or the government? Only time will tell, for the proof of the pudding is in the eating.

7

Good Governance

The Modi government's track record has thus far been a mixed bag of hits and controversies. Modi's view on governance is captured in the slogan *Minimum Government and Maximum Governance* – a key message in his party's election manifesto in 2014 and again in 2019.

By and large, the Modi government has been able to provide an incorruptible administration.[73] None of his ministers or associated bureaucrats has been charged with any major scams.[74] This may be due to the Modi government's zero-tolerance approach to corruption and black money. Some may attribute it to Modi's style of functioning, that is, his preference to work closely with bureaucrats rather than ministers, and his efforts to make the bureaucracy more efficient, performance-oriented, and accountable.

Putting its house in order first

Reforming the Indian civil services is one of the top priorities of the Modi government, for this lies at the core of good governance.[75]

The moniker given to the Indian civil services – 'the steel frame of India' – suggests its importance in administering the country but also how resistant it is to alterations. As civil servants are extremely powerful within the machinations of government, any change that undermines their authority or reduces their benefits is met with stiff resistance. Reforms that do go through are undone or diluted over time. However, the Modi government has made some significant inroads in this context.

One of its first actions was to remove the mandatory requirement of prior sanction to prosecute civil servants, a feature that stripped any sense of legal protection available to them. The government has made its stance very clear – it aims to ensure probity among public servants while protecting them from frivolous allegations.

This was followed by the removal of 'red beacons' or '*lal battis*' atop of cars – the only vestige of authority and prestige available to civil servants in the field. The larger purpose behind it was to do away with the country's colonial inheritance. This applied to all ministers and indeed to PM Modi himself too.

Further, the Modi government prematurely retired 340 non-performing officers from July 2014 to December 2020.[76] This is not a new undertaking; previous governments have taken similar steps in the past. The rules have provisions to retire a government employee prematurely for allegedly being corrupt and non-performance, among others. Although not new, the scale of it is definitely something that sets the Modi government apart from its predecessors.

Some states are following suit. For example, the Haryana government recently laid off an IAS officer for corruption, who had been under suspension since 2016 after a CBI court found him guilty of amassing assets disproportionate to his declared income. The officer in question is only the second IAS officer from the state to be dismissed for corruption. Hopefully, this current enthusiasm of the states will last long enough to leave an abiding impact on the administration.[77]

Alongside these tough measures, the Modi government has been working towards making the bureaucracy more efficient, performance-oriented, and accountable. It has taken several steps in this regard. One, the department of personnel introduced the new practice of conducting a 360-degree investigation of a bureaucrat's career before promoting them to the position of secretary to the Government of India, the highest rung for a civil servant.

Two, the government has opened the doors for professionals to join the top echelons of bureaucracy by recruiting nearly 40 officials at the level of joint secretary from the private sector. These officials have been introduced to plug the talent deficit and transform the work culture of the civil services, which is hamstrung by red tape. In its first term, the Modi administration's initial attempts at absorbing officers through lateral entry didn't meet with much success, presumably due to the delay tactics of some officers. In response, the government moved the process from the Department of Personnel and Training and entrusted it to the Union Public Service Commission (UPSC). At the end of its first term, the Modi government could induct only nine officers through this channel. It made another push to induct 30 more private-sector specialists to different government departments at the crucial decision-making level of joint secretaries and directors on a contract basis. This time around, right from the beginning, UPSC was put in the driver's seat while selecting candidates.[78] The process worked smoothly.

Three, the government has broken the structures that promoted silos between departments. For example, the National Academy of Administration in Mussoorie – a training institute exclusively for IAS officers – has been opened to non-IAS officers too. Additionally, IAS officers are now being imparted mid-career training alongside non-IAS officers.[79] To provide them with a common base, all the probationers of the All India Services (AIS) together receive foundational course training.[80] These steps will go a long way in enabling officers to work seamlessly across departments. At the same time, it will help the government leverage a common pool of talent.[81] The government has started putting young IAS recruits through probationary stints in the Prime Minister's Office (PMO) too.

Another big reform is the speeding-up of decision-making within the bureaucracy. The Modi government is in the process of introducing a measure that will ensure that any given file passes through no more than four hands while making any decision. PM Modi believes that a civil servant's role is less about giving orders and more about ensuring that the country stays on the right path in the face of changes. For this, a civil servant needs to stay connected with common citizens so that they can understand their problems.

The Modi government has also instituted a mechanism to periodically review progress on ongoing development projects. PRAGATI (Pro-Active Governance and Timely Implementation) is used to monitor/review important projects and programmes of the central government in addition to projects flagged by state governments. PRAGATI meeting, an ICT-based platform, brings together the secretaries of the GOI and the states' chief secretaries.[82]

There have been instances where PM Modi has pulled up officers for delays in the implementation of projects. In one instance, PM Modi lashed out at civil servants three times in the short span of three weeks for the slow pace of work. He also publicly reprimanded the Indian Civil Service (ICS) during his motion of thanks address in the Lok Sabha. He is probably the first PM who hasn't shied away from rebuking civil servants.[83] The government has been keen to achieve targets within timelines as delays result in losses to the exchequer.[84] Through enhanced monitoring and improvements in processes and procedures, it is trying to control delays in project execution.

Other dimensions of governance

There are several other dimensions to the government. For instance, its relationship with (i) civil society, (ii) the business community, and (iii) different levels of government. One commonality among the three dimensions is the extensive use of digital technology to improve governance.

Governance and the civil society

In dealing with civil society, some examples of improved governance stand out – for example, the establishment of common service centres (CSCs). CSCs are access points for the delivery of essential public services such as utility services, social welfare schemes, and a host of services in healthcare, finance, education, and agriculture. In addition, these centres provide a wide variety of services for citizens in rural and remote areas, including issuing caste and birth certificates, licenses, ration cards, PAN cards, land records, banking, bill payments, and so on. These services are now provided digitally by private entrepreneurs at the CSCs who charge a commission for their services.

The CSC intervention was started by the UPA administration under the National e-Governance Plan using the public–private partnership model to make it sustainable way back in 2008. By 2014, when it handed the reins over to the NDA government, it had established nearly 100,000 centres.[85] The Modi government has not only expanded the reach of such centres to cover 2.5 lakh gram panchayats, but it has also expanded the range of services provided, all of which are accessible through a universal technology platform.

Another good example of improved governance is Direct Benefit Transfers (DBTs), that is, the transfer of benefits directly to the bank accounts of beneficiaries. This has been made possible through three independent initiatives: Jan Dhan Yojana (opening of zero-balance bank accounts in public-sector banks for the poor), Aadhar enrolment (assigning a 12-digit unique identification number to every individual in the country), and increasing the prevalence of mobile phones (using them as a means of communication between the government and citizens). Government subsidies under programmes such as PAHAL (benefit to users of LPG cylinders), MGNREGA (employment guarantee), and NSAP (social assistance) are now transferred through DBT. This JAM trinity has improved governance by eliminating leakages and is expected to form the bedrock of many future initiatives.

Using technology to make entitlements under different public programmes portable is yet another means of improving governance. For example, under its One Nation One Ration Card (ONOC) programme, the government has ensured that citizens can seamlessly access the public distribution system across states. Migrants holding a ration card benefit from the programme as they can now access food provisions at any fair price store located anywhere in India (instead of just in the state where the card is registered). This programme spans a cluster of 32 states and UTs and covers about 69 crore beneficiaries. Likewise, the beneficiaries of the government-sponsored health insurance programme – Pradhan Mantri Jan Arogya Yojana – can access healthcare at empanelled government and private hospitals almost anywhere in the country.

Another case in point is the depoliticization of the National (Padma) Awards. In the past, governments have been accused of favouritism and lobbying for Padma awardees. Between 2005 and 2014, on average, 25 persons from Delhi were given the award every year. In 2017, however, only five awardees were chosen from Delhi and not a single doctor from an elite Delhi hospital made it to the list – which usually features many such individuals. Now, the selection is based on a review consisting of multiple stages, and innovators and those rendering selfless services to society are emphasized. True to its word, the government has transformed the Padma awards into the 'People's Padma'.

Governance and the business community

The government is also using technology to reform governance and thereby improve ease of business. For example, in 2017, the government introduced the technology-driven Goods and Services Tax (GST) system, which is the biggest tax reform in Indian taxation history. GST replaced multiple taxes with a single, destination-based tax on the supply of goods and services from the manufacturer to the consumer. GST is a game-changer as it makes it possible to have standardized rates across goods and services, creating a common base. It also makes it possible to have similar rates across states and between the centre and states. While the GST rollout met with some implementation challenges, the government has been taking steps to simplify the system and make it transparent. The GST system has facilitated better tax administration, improved tax compliance, and helped avoid double taxation while ensuring adequate tax collection from inter-state sales.

Similarly, the government made direct tax administration more efficient by introducing an anonymous assessment system in October 2019 for taxpayers who receive IT scrutiny assessment notices. In the new system, assessment cases are randomly allocated by an automated system. Taxpayers receive communications electronically, and the identity of assessing officers remains anonymous. The Income Tax Department is combining technological tools with innovative practices to enhance transparency, improve efficiency, and standardize procedures. Of more than 6 crore returns filed annually, around 300,000 are scrutinized based on select risk parameters. Based on the number of cases scrutinized, this reform may seem small, but it has a significant effect in empowering taxpayers and altering their perception of tax administration.

These tax measures may have left some civil servants utterly disappointed. The prospect of making 'additional' money may have been the motivation, at least in part, for their joining the services. To continue to attract the best talent to the civil services, the salaries and perks of civil servants need to be at par with their counterparts in the private sector.

Ease of doing business (EDB) – a ranking system introduced by the World Bank Group – ranks countries based on their regulatory frameworks in terms of ease of starting and operating businesses. The EDB in India has consistently and significantly improved over the last few years. India has successively scaled greater heights in the index, jumping from 142 in 2014 to 63 in 2019.[86] Higher rankings indicate better, usually simpler, regulations for businesses and stronger protections of property rights.[87] As per the latest World Bank report, India is among the top ten improvers in the world. The time taken to get a business up and running has been reduced from 30 days in 2014 to just 18 days as of 2019. India would have moved further up in this ranking had the World Bank not stopped publishing its report.[88]

Further improvements in EDB are possible in areas such as implementing single-window clearance systems, quicker land acquisition, and readiness to roll out new labour codes. States have a greater role to play as these areas fall within their purview.

In corporate governance too, there has been a distinct improvement. For example, the government has been proactive in identifying and striking off shell companies. It has identified more than 2,38,00 companies as shell companies in the last three years alone.[89]

Governance and tiers of government

The relationship between the centre and non-BJP ruled states is generally marked by differences and tensions. This is true even in the management of the COVID crisis, which required a "whole of government" approach. However, there is more to the centre–state relationship than meets the eye, for the interaction between the two tiers is often guided by multiple considerations including development and politics.

In 2015, the government replaced the Planning Commission with NITI (National Institution for Transforming India) Aayog, which, among other things, is supposed to foster cooperative federalism by involving states in the economic policy-making process. The extent to which it has succeeded is unclear, but one aspect in which NITI Aayog has been successful is in generating competition among states. It has constructed a few indices to rank states' performances in selected areas. This exerts greater pressure on states to perform. These include the SDG India Index, India Innovation Index, Aspirational Districts Programme, and so forth. The overall performance of NITI Aayog is currently under review by a committee consisting of people with impeccable credentials.

Discussion

Some commentators who look at governance from a broader perspective – as inclusive of democracy, individual liberties, and autonomy of public institutions – argue that governance has weakened under the Modi administration. They cite several instances in support of their argument. For example, they argue that the role of the Parliament has been reduced to a mere rubber stamp as significant bills are passed without sufficient discussion. Further, there have been attempts to silence the opposition, lower the quality of debates, skip pre-legislative consultations, refer fewer bills to standing committees for detailed scrutiny, and so forth.[90]

They cite other examples to indicate that certain moves of the Modi government run counter to the spirit of good governance; for instance, by compromising the functioning of public institutions, appointing heads of public institutions not based on merit and seniority but politics, diluting laws (e.g., Right to Information Act), disregarding processes, practices, rules, and procedures, compromising centre–state relations, and so on.

While there may be some truth to all of this, the same can be viewed from a different perspective. For example, when opposition parties stop playing a constructive role in the Parliament, resorting to 'certain' methods may be justifiable.

Similarly, outside of politics, when professionals or bureaucrats need to be compulsorily retired on the grounds of non-performance or corruption, resorting to harsh methods and stringent actions may be necessary to move things forward.

Indeed, the Modi government has made several 'enemies' from all walks of life over the last few years – be it politics, the corporate sector, professional associations, the civil services, the media, civil society, etc. These critics also include people being held accountable for their past misdeeds or who stand to lose 'rent-seeking' – those who seek to gain wealth without any productive contribution.

Even though they are a minority, when these critics are resourceful – well-funded and well-connected – they pose a potential danger to the government. The 'deterioration' in governance under the Modi leadership may be a response to deal with the new 'lows' seen in different walks of life.

So, there are both arguments and counterarguments with regards to the Modi government's performance on governance interpreted broadly. However, the fact that there have been some solid gains on certain key dimensions of governance cannot be denied.

8

Narendra Damodardas Modi

This book will remain incomplete if we do not discuss Modi himself – specifically, his personality and style of functioning. A lot has already been said about his qualities – that he is a great leader and visionary, confident, decisive, and charismatic. This chapter doesn't dwell on any of these. Instead, it analyses Modi's personality and style through the lens of economic development.

Modi – a man of all seasons

PM Modi is passionate, ambitious, and strategic about development. Therefore, he takes an active interest in a wide range of issues, sets ambitious goals such as converting India into a $5 trillion economy and doubling farmers' incomes, and pursues sweeping economic reforms such as the GST and the Insolvency and Bankruptcy Code.

His entrepreneurial spirit allows for opportunism and the exploration of new vistas, helping him turn even crises like the COVID-19 pandemic into an opportunity for improvement.

He has the mindset of a businessman, which allows him to understand the value of money as well as the significance of taking action. Even the gifts he receives as PM are being monetized through auctions, the proceeds of which are put towards conserving the Ganges – something that has never been done before. So far, there have been three rounds of auctions that have evoked huge interest among the public.

The fact that Modi is a tough negotiator was publicly acknowledged by none other than the former US President, Donald Trump, in the context of the US–India trade deal, which didn't go through.[91] This was also noted during the final negotiations of the long-overdue Regional Comprehensive Economic Partnership (RCEP) – a free trade agreement (FTA) among Asia-Pacific nations. India withdrew from RCEP at the eleventh hour after days of prolonged negotiation at the ASEAN summit because it felt that the proposed agreement didn't accommodate some of its core interests. As with an industrious personality, he has stated on record that he will create a new paradigm of hard work.[92] He understands the need to constantly keep his foot on the pedal, especially when targets are ambitious and the development journey is arduous – a trait that draws awe and respect from the people around him.

He is strong-willed and resolute when he is convinced of something. Yet, he is flexible when the situation so warrants. Modi stepped back from three farm bills his government got the Parliament to pass in 2020 after protests erupted in the states of Uttar Pradesh, Haryana, and Punjab. He gave it his best shot but was also willing to bow to the will of the people. Modi understands the bitter price that must be paid to keep reforms moving.

He is inclusive in matters of development, connecting with all sections of society – teachers, students, the differently-abled, tribals, street vendors, sportspersons, healthcare workers, taxpayers, and so forth. Development programmes organized by his government are non-discriminatory and some are aimed at complete (100 per cent) saturation – electrification, housing, toilet coverage, etc. If anything, he has been giving special attention to neglected areas, whether it is geographic regions, population subgroups, or development issues.

PM Modi loves doing things at scale: constructing the world's tallest statue (Statue of Unity), conducting the world's largest exercise in crowd management (during Kumbh Mela 2019 in Prayagraj),[93] getting the UN to proclaim an International Yoga Day (June 21st), laying the foundation of the world's largest Hindu temple (Ram Mandir in Ayodhya, Uttar Pradesh), running the world's largest vaccination drive, and so on. Many development programmes that were initiated by the UPA government such as CSCs and health insurance for the poor have also been scaled up.

To add to this, he is quick to learn from his mistakes. For instance, the demonetization of higher currency notes did not yield the expected results. However, his government was quick to promote digital transactions and used the intel gathered from the exercise to locate potentially fraudulent companies and individuals. He has always seen failure as an opportunity to learn and encourages others to subscribe to the same view. This was evident in his response to the failure of India's first-ever fencer, CA Bhavani Devi, to secure a medal for India in the Tokyo Olympics. Modi not only consoled her but also offered words of encouragement; he responded the same way to the ISRO Chandrayaan-2's mission failure to soft-land the Vikram lander on the moon in 2019.

In an age where technological innovations are creating disruptions in almost every domain, it is important to leverage new ideas. Modi is open to experimentation, well demonstrated by the Light House Projects (LHPs), meant to showcase different modern technologies and innovative processes in the construction of houses. Using technologies from different countries, LHP is being implemented in six Indian cities: Indore (Madhya Pradesh), Rajkot (Gujarat), Chennai (Tamil Nadu), Ranchi (Jharkhand), Agartala (Tripura), and Lucknow (Uttar Pradesh). New technologies will reduce construction time and make houses more resilient, affordable, and comfortable.

PM Modi also seamlessly adapts to situations. At times he speaks like a statesman, and at others, a street-smart politician. He sounds strikingly different during his monthly radio programme, Mann Ki Baat, compared to his addresses at election rallies. Some political commentators have even said that his election speeches are unbecoming of a PM! Sometimes, when recounting history, he sounds as if he is steeped in the past; at other times, when talking about emerging technologies, he sounds futuristic. Similarly, sometimes he seems scientific, and at others, superstitious. On the one hand, he promotes products or programmes based on modern science, and on the other hand, he plumps for pseudoscience. All of this only suggests that he has no fixed approach. He adapts to situations and deploys strategies to his advantage.

On his style of decision-making

There is a famous African proverb, "If you want to go fast, go alone. If you want to go far, go together." PM Modi wants to go far and fast simultaneously, and he can do it due to his inimitable style. So, what is his style?

Firm grip on the development agenda

All decision-making power is highly centralized in his office so much so that some people refer to him as an autocrat or even a dictator. However, he has his ear to the ground and receives inputs from different sources, which enables him to develop a sound understanding of issues at the grassroots level. He has a rounded view of development and can guide his team towards reasonably good solutions.

Although some observers are critical of the centralization of power, there may be good reasons for it.[94] One, it helps create a clean administration. Creating several power points can potentially be detrimental to his zero-tolerance approach to corruption. Two, to have a firm grip on the development agenda and steer it forward with speed, quality, and consistency, centralization is helpful. Three, it helps prevent his ministerial colleagues or officers from playing into vested interests, which can potentially undermine the government. Four, to advance brand Modi. Fortunately for him, having an absolute majority in Parliament allows him the luxury of centralization of power.

Actions speak louder than words

Modi is a man of action or *karmyogi*. In a country with a huge development deficit but not a discussion deficit, the government's focus is clear – to take action. A famous dialogue from the 1966 English movie *The Good, the Bad and the Ugly* is quite opportune here.[95] The analogous statement would be "When you have to act, act, don't talk!" Indeed, it's time to act to advance India's development.

One may argue that discussion could improve the quality of decision-making. While true, clearing the backlog of projects must take precedence over argumentation and debate. Additionally, decision-making can be a long-drawn-out process in a country like

India. For instance, several people heavily critiqued the GST rollout, but had the project slowed down, it would have lost the momentum it needed to be successful.

Doesn't reveal his cards all at once

Analysing the Modi government's development interventions is best done holistically. Take, for example, Jan Dhan Yojana – it was thought to be a programme aimed at financial inclusion alone. Similarly, scaling up Aadhar registration and promoting mobile apps were thought to concern digital identities and communication channels, respectively, but the combination of all of these interventions is what enabled Direct Benefit transfers (DBT) under several government programmes, which has proved to be a gamechanger.

People need to exercise patience to understand the gradual unfolding of Modi's development vision. For example, in 2018, when the Modi government launched an ambitious health insurance scheme, Pradhan Mantri Jan Arogya Yojana (PMJAY), for nearly 50 crore Indians from lower-income households, some experts criticized it on varied grounds. A well-known development economist and a social activist, Jean Drèze, was quick to criticize the budget allocations made to PMJAY.[96] Had he been aware of what was coming, he probably would have been cautious with his criticism.

The element of surprise

Springing surprises on people – be it fellow parliamentarians or specific sections of society or the public – has been an important part of his toolkit. Demonetization of higher currency notes, imposition of complete lockdown during the coronavirus pandemic, the withdrawal of the three farm bills, etc. were announced suddenly and without warning. An element of surprise in parliamentary business helps the government catch the opposition off-guard. At other times, it is meant to bring parity in the implementation of government decisions.

Although Modi is a dynamic decision-maker who constantly evaluates his strategies and builds on them, the opposition and the public are getting more and more familiar with his style. In a context where the opposition is up in arms against him and doesn't mind derailing his development agenda, it remains to be seen to what extent he can continue using this strategy.

Power of symbolic gestures

In matters of economic development, Modi has been a man of substance, but he also understands the value of symbolic gestures.

He is not afraid to make little gestures to win the hearts and minds of specific communities for the larger purpose of development. For example, he made an unscheduled visit to Gurudwara Rakab Ganj Sahib in Delhi on the eve of Guru Tegh Bahadur's death anniversary. Wearing culturally appropriate clothing, he paid tribute to the Guru for his supreme sacrifice. His visit assumed special significance as it came at a time of intense protests by farmers, especially from Punjab, against the three farm laws enacted by his government.

Modi's style of functioning is such that it gets acknowledged and occasionally lauded, even by those belonging to the opposition camp. For example, the Nationalist Congress Party president, Sharad Pawar, said that once PM Modi takes up any task, he makes sure it is completed. Further, Mr. Pawar noted that PM Modi puts in a lot of effort and gives ample time to get things done. And that he has a good hold on his administration.[97]

The Modi government's broad-based and fast-paced development strategy for India is meant to unlock India's economic potential. In his scheme of things, all sections of society must contribute to, as well as benefit from, India's growth story.

Increasingly, he is making economic development his most potent tool to win over citizens.

For a long time now, India has needed a prime minister with a strong personality to realize its potential. The absence of this has led to a slow pace of development that gave critics reason to crib. Paradoxically, some of them still do!

9

Concluding Thoughts

The Modi government has stirred the nation like no other. While the overall track record has been mixed, when we consider the development front alone, it has performed reasonably well. In addition to expanding previous development initiatives by the UPA government, the Modi government has been strengthening traditional growth drivers and opening new vistas of growth. The government is counting a great deal on women and youth to drive India's future growth, as well as on technological innovations that are promising new and affordable solutions. Alongside making systemic corrections and building new foundations, the government is designing development interventions with a long-term horizon. However, the effects of their performance will be only visible from the medium term, which attracts criticism from those who fail to see the big picture.

Outside of economic development, however, there are several reasons to be critical of the Modi government across the domains of politics, civil liberties, and management of central agencies. The government has made compromises in these non-economic domains both to achieve its political ambitions and quell the opposition.

Achieving political ambitions

The NDA-led Modi government has an unsatiated thirst for political power. It plays dirty tricks and makes compromises to acquire power. Yet, Modi – on record – has said that he is not power-hungry. This may be true in the sense that his party seeks political power, not for the sake of power but to be able to pursue long-term economic development. According to Modi, politics is the means to pursue development and is subservient to realizing development.

Quelling the opposition

Unlike time that only moves in one direction, development can go both ways. A country can progress or regress on the development front. Advancing development is one thing, protecting it from regression is another. When certain individuals or groups start working against the country's economic interests, certain measures have to be taken. A politician or a party eyeing to grab power may undermine the government's progress in furthering development, and businesspeople hurt by reforms can form a coalition to pose roadblocks. Countering such activities, in turn, may call for harsh or even repressive measures. Bypassing rules and clamping on liberties is justified if it is in the larger interest of the nation. If state agencies need to be controlled in the interest of development, it may be a regrettable necessity.

Development is sacrosanct to the Modi government. In a distorted world like ours, development can hardly be delivered with clinical precision. That is, it cannot be realized without errors or compromises, given the number of obstacles in the way of efficient decision-making in the country. Additionally, the government is as opportunistic with politics as it is with development – another source of criticism.

Those who value the means as much as the ends have reasons to be critical of the Modi government. Those to whom progress in non-economic domains is at least as important as improvements in the development domain will be sceptical. Those who believe that the extent of compromises being made in non-economic domains is too heavy a price to advance development will also be disapproving. Nonetheless, to negate or belittle what the Modi government has accomplished on the development front is incorrect.

Seeing the compromises made in non-development domains, some people are quick to voice their reproval. These critics need to remind themselves of situations when development itself gets compromised, genuine reforms get delayed by politicking, and development opportunities are left untapped due to distracted leadership. Who raises their voice then?

Over the years, development has been held hostage to petty politics. For example, it took almost seven years for India to open up its insurance sector to private competition. Should it have taken that long? The Malhotra Committee submitted its report in January 1994 arguing in favour of private competition. However, the reforms were introduced only in 2000. It took several years of discussion and debate for the reforms to be implemented, and not all of it was carried through with good intent. Whoever was in the opposition (including the then BJP), mindful of who would get credited, used delay tactics, opposing the bills in Parliament on some pretext or the other. Where were all the critics then?

Many stalled infrastructure projects such as the Kundli–Manesar–Palwal expressway and Kashi Vishwanath corridor project – which had been on hold for over a decade – have now been completed and delivered by the Modi government without fuss or fanfare, raising the bar for future governments.

In the view of the Modi government, economic development takes precedence over other forms of development. Further, when the process of introducing reforms takes exceedingly long in the face of impatient citizenry, it considers it to be its moral right to take shortcuts. When there are delays in decision-making, the government may bypass or override processes and protocols. Compromising on development processes may be an inescapable necessity to speed up development. Isn't fast-paced development one of the hallmarks of the Modi government?

In a large and heterogeneous country like India, advancing development can be tough. Scaling development interventions requires huge resources – financial and operational – that are not easy to muster. Additionally, if development is broad-based, as opposed to it being confined to small geographies, progress can be sluggish. The Modi government may have faltered in achieving some of its ambitious goals as per its timelines and there may be scope for further improvement in programmes that have been implemented; still, what has been achieved so far is no small feat.

Modi is known for thinking big, for doing things at scale – whether it is in politics or the development arena. While the 'scale effect' in politics may be vicious, the same turns virtuous when applied to the development front. While BJP's politics in the era of Modi may be cause for some concern, its progress in terms of development so far has been noteworthy, with some of its initiatives even being extraordinary!

After all, while it may be beautiful, even the lotus has its roots in muddy water!

****

End Notes

1. Under a national program, Ek Bharat Shreshtha Bharat, launched on October 31, 2015.
2. The lotus flower is the symbol of BJP.
3. In north India, these were largely based on collective faith and caste, sub-caste, and sub-sub-caste identities, while in south India, these were usually founded on sub-regional appeals.
4. News 18, "'Majoritarianism Leading India Down a Dark Path': Raghuram Rajan on 'Worrisome' Situation," October 12, 2019, https://www.news18.com/news/india/majoritarianism-leading-india-down-a-dark-path-raghuram-rajan-says-economy-in-a-worrisome-situation-2343629.html.
5. The Economic Times, "Election Commission of India Not in Favour of State Funding of Elections", March 2, 2020, https://economictimes.indiatimes.com/news/politics-and-nation/election-commission-of-india-not-in-favour-of-state-funding-of-elections/articleshow/74440756.cms.
6. Yogesh Sapkale, "SBI Sold Electoral Bonds Worth Rs 6,492.7 Crore in 3 Years, with BJP Being the Biggest Beneficiary: Analysis", National Herald, Jan 4, 2021, https://www.nationalheraldindia.com/india/sbi-sold-electoral-bonds-worth-rs-64927-crore-in-3-years-with-bjp-being-the-biggest-beneficiary-analysis.
7. Shreejit Shelar, "Rahul Gandhi Claims BJP Holds 'Absolute Financial and Media Dominance' in the Country", Business Upturn, April2, 2021, https://

www.businessupturn.com/politics/rahul-gandhi-claims-bjp-holds-absolute-financial-and-media-dominance-in-the-country/
8. The Hindu, "44% of MLAs who Switched Parties Joined the BJP: ADR Report", March 12, 2021, https://www.thehindu.com/news/national/44-of-mlas-who-switched-parties-joined-bjp-adr-report/article34043428.ece.
9. Sridhar Acharyulu, "The Government Is SLAPPing Down and Intimidating Central Information Commissioners", The Wire, Dec 5, 2018, https://thewire.in/government/cic-rti-narendra-modi-government.
10. The Times of India, "PM Asked Me Why I Wasn't Letting Bills Be Passed Amid Din: Hamid Ansari in Book", Jan 28, 2021, https://timesofindia.indiatimes.com/india/pm-asked-me-why-i-wasn't-letting-bills-be-passed-amid-din-hamid-ansari-in-book/articleshowprint/80490232.cms.
11. The Wire, "In Unprecedented Move, Modi Government Sends Former CJI Ranjan Gogoi to Rajya Sabha", 16 March, 2020, https://thewire.in/law/cji-ranjan-gogoi-rajya-sabha-nomination.
12. It is advice to rulers or administrators on how to get a task done by someone who is not inclined to do it. It's a part of Chanakya NITI offered to the then ruling dynasty of the Mauryas in the 4th century BCE.
13. The Hindu, "Balakot Air Strike, 10% Quota and Farmers' Scheme Gave Modi Govt a Boost: Survey", April 8, 2019, https://www.thehindu.com/elections/lok-sabha-2019/higher-support-for-modi-government-following-recent-decisions-survey/article26735746.ece.
14. India's GDP stood at $2.7 trillion in 2018.
15. Department of Economic Affairs, Ministry of Finance, 2019, Economic Survey 2018–19, Government of India, https://www.indiabudget.gov.in/budget2019-20/economicsurvey/doc/echapter.pdf.
16. Telegraph India, "Chidambaram Delinks $5-trillion Target and Prime Ministership," July 12, 2019, https://www.telegraphindia.com/india/chidambaram-delinks-5-trillion-target-and-prime-ministership/cid/1694337.
17. Business Insider, "Modi's $5 Trillion Dream Is Wishful Thinking Says Former PM Manmohan Singh," February 20, 2020, https://www.businessinsider.in/india/news/modis-5-trillion-dream-is-wishful-thinking-says-former-pm-manmohan-singh/articleshow/74219221.cms.
18. Business Today, "PM Slams 'Professional Pessimists', Says India Poised to Become $5-trillion Economy by 2024", July 6, 2019, PM slams 'professional

pessimists', says India poised to become $5-trillion economy by 2024 - BusinessToday.

19. Business Standard, "Modi Govt's $5-trn GDP Target Looks Ambitious, Says Economist R Nagaraj," January 13, 2020, https://www.business-standard.com/article/economy-policy/modi-govt-s-5-trillion-gdp-target-by-2024-looks-unimaginably-ambitious-120011200682_1.html.

20. According to the newly appointed chief economic advisor, V Anantha Nageswaran, India may become $5 trillion economy by 2025-26 or 2026-27.

21. As measured by the share in GDP of gross expenditure on R&D (GERD). In 1996, this share for China and India was 0.6 percent and 0.64 percent respectively. In 2020, this share for China had risen to 2.4 percent while for India it had remained below 0.8 percent.

22. Dept. for Promotion of Industry and Internal Trade, Ministry of Commerce and Trade, "Evolution of Startup India: Capturing the Five Year Story", Government of India. https://www.startupindia.gov.in/content/dam/invest-india/Templates/public/5_years_Achievement_report%20_%20PRINT.pdf.

23. NITI Aayog, Government of India, "About WEP," https://wep.gov.in/about-wep.

24. Manish Kumar, "The 3 Challenges to Skill Development in India – and How to Tackle Them," We Forum, October 1, 2019, https://www.weforum.org/agenda/2019/10/india-skill-development-programme/

25. The policy proposes that students from class 6 onwards have the option of selecting a course in line with their interests and local needs and business. Also, it proposes an integration of academic and vocational subjects at the intermediate or middle level. How quickly this integration happens remains to be seen.

26. As on August 2, 2021.

27. Mani Juneja, "Blue Economy: An Ocean of Livelihood Opportunities in India," The Energy Resources Institute< March 12, 2021, https://www.teriin.org/article/blue-economy-ocean-livelihood-opportunities-india.

28. News Services Division, "Parliament Passes Inland Vessels Bill," All India Radio, August 2, 2021, https://newsonair.gov.in/News?title=Parliament-passes-Inland-Vessels-Bill%2c-2021&id=423291.

29. Currently, India spends more than 12 lakh crore on the import of energy.

30. News Services Division, "Morning News," All India Radio, August 13, 2021, https://newsonair.gov.in/Text-Bulletin-Details.aspx?id=37282.

31. Vibhuti Garg, "IEEFA: No Excuses, India Must Ramp up Solar Manufacturing to Reduce Reliance on Imports," Institute for Energy Economics and Financial Analysis, July 19, 2021, https://ieefa.org/ieefa-no-excuses-india-must-ramp-up-solar-manufacturing-to-reduce-reliance-on-imports/.
32. As it can be extracted from sugarcane, damaged food grains, and agricultural waste.
33. The government had a plan of raising the share to 20% by 2030. Going by the current rate, the government has advanced the target date for achieving 20% blending from 2030 to 2025.
34. Hydrogen is designated by different colours, depending on how it is produced. For example, hydrogen produced using fossil fuel is called black hydrogen. Similarly, hydrogen produced using energy from nuclear power sources is called pink hydrogen.
35. Pritam Singh, "Green Hydrogen, a New Ally for a Zero-carbon Future," The Hindu, September 9, 2021,
36. News Services Division, "India has potential to become global hub of green hydrogen in near future: Dr Jitendra Singh," All India Radio, Sept 4, 2021, https://newsonair.gov.in/News?title=India-has-potential-to-become-global-hub-of-green-hydrogen-in-near-future%3a-Dr-Jitendra-Singh&id=425444.
37. News Services Division, "Morning News," All India Radio, September 8, 2021, https://newsonair.gov.in/Text-Bulletin-Details.aspx?id=37508.
38. India has 151 GW of renewables and 6.7 GW of nuclear. Government of India, "Power Sector at a Glance: All India," https://powermin.gov.in/en/content/power-sector-glance-all-India.
39. Even for countries like India that rely heavily on coal power, lifetime emissions for battery electric vehicles are lower (by 19% to 34%) compared to that of gasoline cars (a study by the International Council on Clean Transportation).
40. News Services Division, "Over 5 Lakh 17 Thousand Electric Vehicles Registered in Country over Last Three Years: Govt," All India Radio, August 10, 2021, https://newsonair.gov.in/News?title=Over-5-lakh-17-thousand-electric-vehicles-registered-in-country-over-last-three-years%3a-Govt&id=423872.
41. Automobile industry accounts for about 35% in the manufacturing sector and is known to be a job multiplier industry.
42. News Services Division, "Govt Committed to Shift Public Transport and Logistics on 100% Green & Clean Sources of Energy: Nitin Gadkari," All India Radio, October 1, 2021, https://newsonair.gov.in/News?title=Govt-

committed-to-shift-public-transport-and-logistics-on-100%25-green-%26-clean-sources-of-energy%3a--Nitin-Gadkari&id=427206.

43 PLIs are for both automobile companies and auto component companies.
44 An economic model designed to minimize resource input, as well as waste and emission production.
45 News Services Division, "Morning News," All India Radio, August 13, 2021, https://newsonair.gov.in/Text-Bulletin-Details.aspx?id=37282
46 EVs will reduce tailpipe emissions, but it will take some time for them to achieve net-zero carbon emissions until electricity generation turns green.
47 Another example of innovative thinking in the existing modes of transportation is using existing broad-gauge lines to run metros rather than building expensive new metro lines.
48 Doubling the income of farmers is an unscientific goal – not because it's unrealistic but because of challenges associated with setting the baseline and the definitional issue as to who qualifies as a farmer: those engaged only in agriculture or in allied activities too. This definitional issue assumes significance as one of the strategies for doubling farm income is diversifying income sources to include activities allied to agriculture such as poultry farming, fisheries, livestock rearing, bee-keeping, and so on.
49 Indian Forest Act of 1927.
50 Press Information Bureau, "100% Neem Coating of Urea Improves Soil Health, Boosts Yields and Curbs Diversion: DACFW Study," Ministry of Chemicals and Fertilizers, Government of India, March 24, 2017, https://pib.gov.in/newsite/printrelease.aspx?relid=159903.
51 The Neem Foundation, "Neem Coated Urea – The Untold Story," https://neemfoundation.org/neem-coated-urea-the-untold-story/.
52 News Services Division, "Text Bulletin Details," All India Radio, October 2, 2021, https://newsonair.gov.in/Text-Bulletin-Details.aspx?id=37726.
53 Ramachandra Guha, "The Exemplary Indian," The Telegraph, February 28, 2022, https://www.telegraphindia.com/opinion/the-exemplary-indian/cid/1830189.
54 The World Bank, "Seamless Transport Connectivity Can Create Major Economic Gains for Bangladesh and India," March 9, 2021, https://www.worldbank.org/en/news/press-release/2021/03/09/seamless-transport-connectivity-can-create-major-economic-gains-for-bangladesh-and-india.
55 News Services Division, "Text Bulletin Details," All India Radio, August 21, 2021, https://newsonair.gov.in/Text-Bulletin-Details.aspx?id=37346.

56 Supporting states in strengthening the primary health care system in the country and in implementing health insurance program – Pradhan Mantri Jan Aarogya Yojana – for around 110 million people households.

57 News Services Division, " Govt to Open 10,000 Pradhan Mantri Bhartiya Janaushadhi Kendras by March 2024," All India Radio, October 13, 2021, https://newsonair.gov.in/News?title=Govt-to-open-10%2c000-Pradhan-Mantri-Bhartiya-Janaushadhi-Kendras-by-March-2024&id=427903.

58 Invest India, "Atmanirbhar Bharat Abhiyaan," National Investment Promotion and Facilitation Agency, https://www.investindia.gov.in/atmanirbhar-bharat-abhiyaan.

59 PM India, "PMs Address to the Nation on 12.5.2020," May 12, 2020, https://www.pmindia.gov.in/en/news_updates/pms-address-to-the-nation-on-12-5-2020/.

60 "Srimad Bhagavadgita Teaches Us How to Serve the World and the People," Narendra Modi, March 9, 2021, https://www.narendramodi.in/prime-minister-s-address-at-release-of-manuscript-on-shlokas-of-srimad-bhagavad-gita-554355.

61 Press Trust of India, "India's Atmanirbhar Abhiyaan Will Make World Order More Just and Fair: President Kovind," January 9, 2021, https://www.republicworld.com/india-news/politics/indias-atmanirbhar-bharat-abhiyaan-will-make-world-order-more-just-and-fair-president-kovind.html.

62 "Congratulating Prime Minister Modi on his Birthday," Dalai Lama, September 17, 2021, https://www.dalailama.com/news/2021/congratulating-prime-minister-modi-on-his-birthday.

63 News Services Division, "India's Achievements are Beneficial Not Only for the Country but also for Entire Humanity, Says PM Modi," All India Radio, March 12, 2021, https://newsonair.gov.in/News?title=India%26%2339%3bs-achievements-are-beneficial-not-only-for-the-country-but-also-for-entire-humanity%2c-says-PM-Modi&id=411634.

64 In his monthly radio programme, Mann Ki Baat, on August 29, 2020, PM Modi urged those interested in raising pet dogs to consider bringing home one of the Indian breeds, some of which are quite beautiful and good. He informed the listeners that some indigenous dog breeds – e.g., Mudhol Hound and Kombi – are so good that they have been trained and inducted into the army.

65 The Indian government has already placed a high-value order with Hindustan Aeronautics Limited (HAL) for the manufacture of the light combat aircraft,

Tejas, for the Indian Air Force. About 500 Indian companies including MSMEs are expected to work with HAL in designing and manufacturing these aircraft. In weapon production too, India is trying to become self-reliant in a couple of years. The government has envisaged a significant role for private players in the sector. It has liberalized the FDI policy in the sector, and the draft Defence Procurement Policy 2020 prioritizes indigenous content.

66 To avoid investing only in China and diversify business into other countries.
67 Karan Bhasin, "Why Atmanirbhar Bharat Should Always be Wary of Import Substitution 2.0," Swarajya, November 5, 2020, https://swarajyamag.com/economy/why-atmanirbhar-bharat-should-always-be-wary-of-import-substitution-20.
68 Tax incentives matter only when companies become profitable while credit incentives often turn into non-performing assets.
69 Firm-level incentives are those that are given to specific firms selected under the scheme. The government then needs to closely monitor the production and sales data of these firms for the determination of incentive payments.
70 Indijval Dasmana, "Rakesh Mohan, Krishnamurthy Subramanian Sing Divergent Tunes on PLI Scheme," The Business Standard, November 19, 2021, https://www.business-standard.com/article/economy-policy/rakesh-mohan-krishnamurthy-subramanian-sing-divergent-tunes-on-pli-scheme-121111900042_1.html.
71 A set of economic policy recommendations for developing countries towards a strongly market-based approach.
72 Import substitution is making an unwelcome comeback, by Douglas A. Irwin. https://www.piie.com/blogs/trade-and-investment-policy-watch/import-substitution-making-unwelcome-comeback.
73 With the exception of the Rafale deal, on which Supreme Court gave an interesting ruling, and the controversy surrounding PM Cares Fund, there has been no major corruption charge against the Modi-led government.
74 The Comptroller and Auditor-General (CAG), in its preliminary findings, raised red flags regarding the Modi government's BharatNet programme, which intends to connect six lakh villages with high-speed internet. The CAG stated that the programme had failed to take off due to financial irregularities (The Hindu, July 18 2021). In the cabinet reshuffle that took place a few days prior to the CAG report going public, the Modi government had removed Ravi Shankar Prasad who had headed the Ministry

	of Electronics and Information Technology when the programme was rolled out. Some commentators believe financial irregularities to be the reason for the shunting of the minister.
75	Reforming the civil service was explicitly mentioned in the party's general election manifesto of 2019.
76	This is based on a written reply by the MOS personnel, Jitendra Singh, to a question in the Rajya Sabha.
77	Dilip Cherian, "With Scindia at Helm, Air India's Divestment Back in Focus," The Asian Age, July 28, 2021, https://www.asianage.com/opinion/columnists/270721/dilip-cherian-with-scindia-at-helm-air-indias-divestment-back-in-focus.html.
78	Dilip Cherian, "Fresh Push for Lateral Entry of Babus Likely," The Asian Age, March 17, 2021, https://www.asianage.com/opinion/columnists/170321/dilip-cherian-fresh-push-for-lateral-entry-of-babus-likely-1.html.
79	This is being done under Mission Karmayogi.
80	Under the 'Aarambh' initiative, an integrated foundation course is taught to probationers of Group-A Central Service and Foreign Service.
81	Dilip Cherian, "Babu's 'Equality'? Mid-career Course at Mussoorie Will Lose IAS-only Tag," The Asian Age, August 25, 2021, https://www.asianage.com/opinion/columnists/250821/babus-equality-mid-career-course-at-mussoorie-will-lose-ias-only-tag.html.
82	PRAGATI is an ICT-based multi-modal platform that bundles three latest technologies: digital data management, video conferencing, and geospatial technology.
83	Arvind Panagariya, India Unlimited: Reclaiming the Lost Glory, February 25, 2020.
84	Aman Sharma, "Exclusive: PM Modi Wants List of Indra Projects Delayed due to Court and NGT Orders, Loss to Exchequer," September 01, 2021, https://www.news18.com/news/india/exclusive-pm-modi-wants-list-of-infra-projects-delayed-due-to-court-and-ngt-orders-loss-to-exchequer-4151015.html.
85	This number is disputed. The Modi government claims that there were around 80,000 such centres in 2014, while this number is believed to be more than 1.2 lakh based on a reply in the Lok Sabha in December 2013 by the then-minister of state in the Prime Minister's office, V Narayanasamy.
86	"Scaling Up in Ease of Doing Business Rankings," Narendra Modi, May 29, 2020, https://www.narendramodi.in/vikasyatra/articledetail/ease-of-doing-business/scaling-up-in-ease-of-doing-business-rankings-547495.

87 Make in India, "Ease of Doing Business," https://www.makeinindia.com/eodb.

88 The World Bank stopped publishing the report due to data irregularities reported to boost China's ranking in 2017.

89 As per the information given by the Minister of State for Corporate Affairs – Rao Inderjit Singh – in a written reply to a question in the Rajya Sabha on July 27, 2021.

90 Jaiveer Shergill, "Opposition is also a People's Mandate. Modi Govt is Decaying Parliamentary Debates," MSN, December 27, 2021, https://www.msn.com/en-in/news/opinion/opposition-is-also-a-people-e2-80-99s-mandate-modi-govt-is-decaying-parliamentary-debates/ar-AASajUt.

91 FPJ Bureau, "Donald Trump Returns Empty Handed, but Not for an Arms Contract that will Benefit US Cos," The Free Press Journal, February 26, 2020, https://www.freepressjournal.in/india/donald-trump-returns-empty-handed-but-for-an-arms-contract-that-will-benefit-us-cos.

92 PR Ramesh, "'It is Important that Every Youngster Get Opportunities, Not Assistance that Keeps them Dependent but the Support that Makes them Self-Reliant to Fulfil their Aspirations with Dignity'," Open, October 2, 2021, https://openthemagazine.com/cover-stories/important-every-youngster-get-opportunities-not-assistance-keeps-dependent-support-makes-self-reliant-fulfil-aspirations-dignity/.

93 Zee News, "Kumbh Mela 2019 Enters Guinness Book of World Records," March 5, 2019, https://zeenews.india.com/uttar-pradesh/kumbh-mela-2019-enters-guinness-book-of-world-records-2185219.html.

94 For example, Raghuram Rajan believes that the centralized structure in the Modi government is hindering economic progress.

95 The dialogue in the movie is, "When you have to shoot, shoot, don't talk!" The Good, the Bad and the Ugly, December 23, 1966.

96 Jean Drèze, "Ayushman Bharat Trivialises India's Quest for Universal Health Care," The Wire, September 24, 2018, https://thewire.in/health/ayushman-bharat-trivialises-indias-quest-for-universal-health-care.

97 Press Trust of India, "Sharad Pawar Says PM Modi has a Key Quality that Manmohan Singh Lacked," NDTV, December 30, 2021, https://www.ndtv.com/india-news/pm-modi-has-good-hold-on-administration-says-ncps-sharad-pawar-2678842.

About The Author

Rajeev Ahuja, Ph.D., is a development economist with over 20 years of work experience. He has served as Senior Economist in Bill & Melinda Gates Foundation, as Economist in the World Bank, and as Senior Research Fellow at Indian Council for Research on International Economic Relations. He had also been a consultant to UNDP, ILO, DFID, and Harvard School of Public Health.

Although his recent work has mostly been in the health sector, he brings a rounded perspective on various development issues. He has published extensively in national and international periodicals. Of late, he has been freelancing and seeking to shape public debate in India through his writings in national dailies.

Another book by the author

Death of a Professional – a fictional account of the life of a middle-aged professional, caught between family and work, who is struggling to make a career jump. He falls out of favour with his female boss after he makes a couple of mistakes. No matter how hard he tries, he finds it difficult to please her. Is he finally able to win over his fastidious manager? Or does his effort take him in the opposite direction, further widening the rift between them? How does all this impact his spouse and two young children? And what of his relationship with colleagues?

Capturing the everyday dynamics of life at home and at work, this novella brings out how our hero navigates workplace challenges, including office politics and tricks that his boss plays. After the highs and lows at work, does he finally get a career jump or face dire consequences?

The book is available online at the Amazon e-book store.

The author would appreciate receiving comments or suggestions at: ahujaahuja@yahoo.com

www.ingramcontent.com/pod-product-compliance
Lightning Source LLC
Chambersburg PA
CBHW071516220526
45472CB00003B/1050

www.ingramcontent.com/pod-product-compliance
Lightning Source LLC
Chambersburg PA
CBHW050207230526
45470CB00001B/283